POPULAR MECHANICS

HOW TO FIX ANYTHING

ESSENTIAL HOME REPAIRS ANYONE CAN DO

HEARST
books

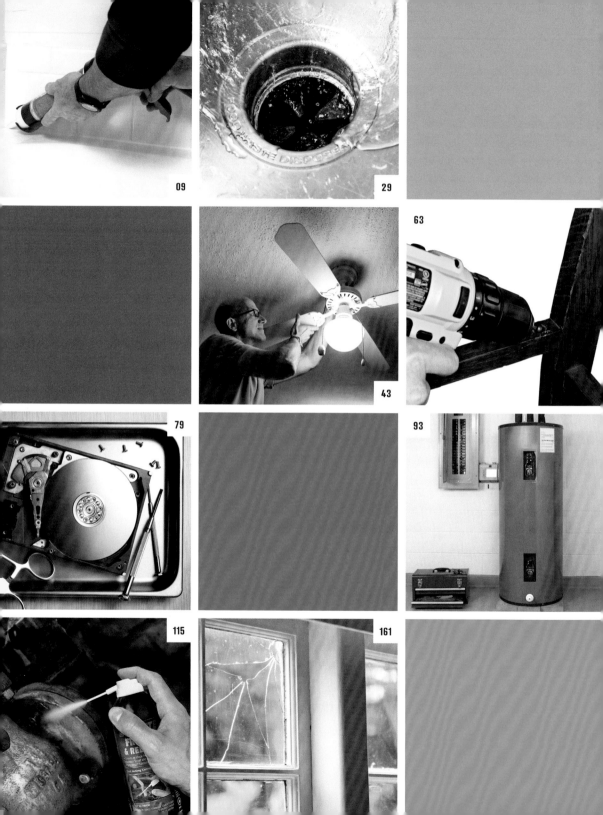

We all want to be capable. We want to be the person who doesn't have to call a handyman every time there's a rip in the screen door or the shower drain makes a funny sound. We want to be a resource for friends and family, offering tools, advice, and the occasional helping hand. Basically, we want to be *Popular Mechanics* Senior Home Editor Roy Berendsohn.

There are a few ways to get there. In Roy's case, you work in cabinetry and construction, then learn on the job as a staff member at *Popular Mechanics* for nearly three decades. That takes a while, as does the option of apprenticing under a plumber, carpenter, and electrician. Or you can take full advantage of the book in your hands. Drawing on *Popular Mechanics*'115-year history of instruction, this book presents solutions to more than 150 common home problems. It is written for everyone, regardless of experience. It should serve as a memory-jog for those who have some training and an easy-to-understand introduction for those who don't.

How you use this book is up to you. You can read it as needed—keeping it on the shelf for emergencies and hitting the index when you need help with a specific problem. Or you can read it all at once, preemptively. Or you can do both. Whatever your situation, we expect this guide to become one of the most-read items on your bookshelf.

Even with all the information packed in *How To Fix Anything*, we know that you'll face challenges not covered in these pages. In those moments, however, you will be more prepared. With this book, you'll have the knowledge and confidence you need to do one of the most important things in home repair: adapt.

The Editors
Popular Mechanics

BATHROOM

01

OLD GROUT

Grout that's crumbling and mildewed is both unattractive and mechanically unsound. A common cause of grout failure is that the installer used too much water in mixing a cement-based material. Also keep in mind that some grouts need to be moist-cured. It's not difficult—all you have to do is mist the tile and grout with water from a spray bottle. A sheet of plastic taped in place and draped over the wall holds in the moisture during the curing process. Other grouts need to be coated with a sealer. And while it's tempting to use an inexpensive, commodity grout when a heavy-duty version is called for, it's false economy. While a 25-pound bag of cement-based grout might cost half as much as a polymer-modified version, complete with antifungus additive, the polymer-modified grout will look better and last longer. The polymer improves the grout's water resistance and makes it more flexible so the grout can withstand temperature fluctuations and wall movement.

Follow these steps to ensure a long-lasting and good-looking grout job

1 Buy enough.
Use one of the many grout calculators or charts online to estimate how much grout you need. Better to have a little too much than not enough.

2 Clean.
Thoroughly remove any mildew and soap scum before cutting grout out of the joints.

3 Remove.
Cut out grout to at least half the depth of the tile.

4 Angle.
Apply the new grout at a 45-degree angle to the tile. Work it thoroughly into the spaces between tiles so there are no air bubbles or gaps.

5 Wipe.
Remove as much excess grout as possible while it's wet. It's easier to do at this stage than when it's dry.

6 Caulk.
Apply a high-quality tub-and-tile sealant where the wall meets the tub and in vertical corners where one wall meets another.

RUNNING TOILET

If the toilet runs continuously in a faint trickle, look to the fill valve—in this case, it's a ball cock, a common valve that uses a float mounted on an arm to shut the valve when the tank water has reached the correct level.

Remove the diaphragm screws and look for sand or mineral grit around the diaphragm seat. Remove this sediment with tweezers **(1)**. If the rubber diaphragm seal is worn, replace it **(2)**. In many cases it's wiser to replace the fill

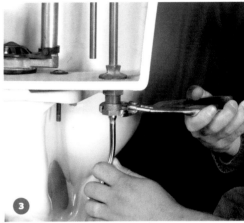

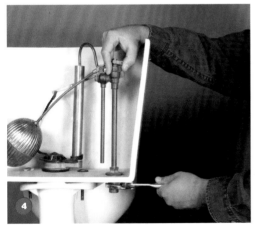

valve than to search for old, discontinued parts. Inexpensive plastic models are reliable and easy to install. Shut off the water, drain the tank completely, and loosen the supply riser's coupling nut (**3**). Next, loosen the ball cock's jamb nut (**4**). Lift the old ball cock from the tank and clean the area around the tank opening. Coat the new fill valve's rubber gasket with Teflon pipe dope and feed its threaded shank through the tank opening (**5**). Tighten the new valve in place and connect the fill line to the top of the overflow tube. Finish by installing a new supply riser between the shut-off valve and the fill valve. Braided stainless steel risers are easiest to use.

TOILET TROUBLESHOOTING

LEAKING TOILET

First, you have to be sure that what you are seeing is a leak and not merely condensation running down the outside of the bowl. Cold water in the toilet and high indoor humidity will result in condensation forming on the outside of the bowl and on the toilet tank. The condensation will accumulate around the bowl's base. There's little that can be done to prevent this. If condensation isn't the cause, you really do have a problem—and sealing the base of the toilet will only make it worse by trapping the moisture at the base of the bowl. Eventually, that can rot out the floor framing. The most likely culprit is a defective wax ring, which should be replaced.

THE TOILET IS ABOUT TO OVERFLOW

As soon as the water level in the bowl starts rising, reach into the tank and prop up the fill valve (the ball or cylinder that floats on top of the water). That will stop the flow to the toilet, thwarting an overflow. Unfortunately you're still going to need the plunger.

A DRIPPING TOILET TANK

This could also just be condensation. To find out if you have a larger problem, put a few drops of food coloring into the tank and see if the color reaches the floor. If it does, check the tank for cracks and the piping for loose connections.

TOILET ROCKS

First, try tightening the hold-down nuts around the base. If that doesn't stop the rocking, you'll have to check the area under the bowl. To do this, shut off and disconnect the water supply, flush the tank, and sponge out residual water. Remove the closet nuts and lift the bowl off the closet bolts.

Three things can be causing the problem. First, the closet flange may be loose or rusted out. Second, the subfloor around the flange may be rotted out, in which case that section needs to be replaced. Finally, the wax ring and its sleeve may be flattened to the extent that it no longer bears properly against the bowl's base, and therefore a new wax ring and sleeve must be installed.

TOILET WON'T FLUSH UNLESS YOU HOLD DOWN THE HANDLE

There is probably too much slack in the lift chain. When you flip the handle, the rubber flapper lifts only slightly off the flush valve seat. The pressure of the water on the flapper causes it to reseat on the flush valve, stopping water flow. By holding the handle for three seconds you are holding the flapper off the valve seat so that the water will flow into the bowl. The water rushing past the flapper holds it up after you release the handle. It also flushes when you snap the handle quickly because the jerky action forces the flapper up to a point where water flowing into the flush valve holds the flapper open.

There are several causes for a slack lift chain. It may be slightly rusted. The hook connecting it to the trip lever may have stretched. Or the flapper may be deteriorating. Whatever the cause, the correction is simple: Eliminate the excessive slack. Do this by moving the chain hook to a different hole on the trip lever or replacing the lift chain. Replace the flapper if it shows excessive wear.

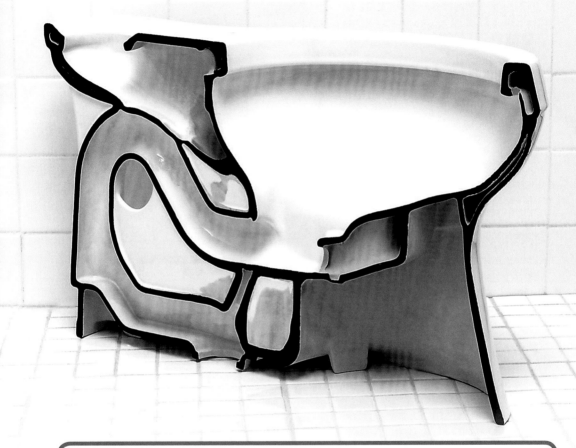

Constantly Flushing Toilet

A worn-out flapper valve is the usual culprit when a toilet sounds as though it's continually flushing itself. Water drains past the leaky valve and triggers the fill valve to admit more water. To replace the flapper, turn off the water supply to the toilet and flush it to drain the water from the tank. Unclip the flapper from the base of the overflow tube, lift it out of the tank, and unhook the chain connecting it to the trip lever. Before you install the new flapper, use a plastic scouring pad to clean the flush valve, where the new flapper will sit when closed. Reattach the chain to the new flapper and clip it in.

DIRTY SHOWER-HEAD

If you notice mineral buildup in the perforations of your showerhead, you can usually dissolve them with white vinegar. The easiest way to accomplish this—which requires no tools—is to fill a Ziploc bag with vinegar, place it around the showerhead, then secure it in place with a rubber band or zip tie. After a few hours, take off the bag and flush the showerhead with water.

FAULTY SHOWER DIVERTER

If you pull up the diverter knob on your bathtub faucet and a good amount of water continues to flow into the tub, don't overreact and cut into the wall. The diverter valve mechanism is inside the tub faucet spout, not inside the wall. The spout is screwed onto the water pipe and can be unscrewed easily. Once the spout is removed, you can see the diverter mechanism. The diverter is a small gate valve attached to the base of the plunger shaft. It is held up (closed position) by water pressure. When the water is turned off, the gate valve drops and opens the tub spout.

If the diverter can't be repaired, it's cheap enough to replace the entire spout, including the diverter mechanism. There are different types and sizes of diverter spouts available, so take your old spout along to the plumbing supply store to make sure you get the right one. Check especially that the set-back distance of the threads within the spout matches the length of your protruding water pipe, so you get a tight fit between the spout shoulder and the wall.

When replacing the spout, use pipe-joint compound on the threads. Fill the hollow back end of the spout with plumbers' putty to prevent water from penetrating the wall.

LOOSE SHOWERHEAD

This typically occurs when the metal strap securing the water-supply pipe pulls free. Here's how to remedy the situation without ripping open the wall. First, pull the round trim ring away from the wall. Next, inject foam sealant into the cavity around the pipe. This stuff expands, so apply it sparingly. Push the trim ring back in place and hold it for a minute or two to contain the foam sealant. The sealant will eventually harden, effectively locking the showerhead in position.

Loose Towel Bar

Remove the bar and use screws to attach it to a clear white pine backboard on which you can route a decorative edge. Paint the backboard to match the existing wall surface or other trim in the room. For a more elegant fix, use nicely finished cherry or oak. Make the backboard long enough to span two studs, then screw it to the wall framing.

DRIPPING FAUCET

When the bathroom faucet springs a leak and it's going to be a few days before you have the time to fix it, the constant dripping can keep you up at night. Give yourself a reprieve by tying a length of string just under the aerator, long enough to rest in the basin. Water runs down the string, and you get peace and quiet.

THE
ESSENTIAL
TOOL

PIPE WRENCH

A pipe wrench may not be versatile, but when you need to hold a pipe and fittings, nothing else will work. The body is rigid and heavy, and the teeth bite forcefully into smooth, round surfaces. While most pipe wrenches are cast iron, spring for an aluminum model if you face a long day of plumbing.

THE AERATOR IS CLOGGED

Aerators serve as low-tech sampling devices—what you find on the aerator can provide valuable information about your water. Blue-green granules on the aerator, for example, indicate water with a high pH (8 or higher). That water is reacting with the aluminum anode in your water heater and releasing aluminum hydroxide into the water system. It collects on the aerator. Replacing the aluminum anode with a magnesium one can help. Rust particles are indicators of rusty steel plumbing that needs replacement. The particles also show up after service disruptions to municipal water systems (such as water-main breaks) or when the water company flushes the system. These organic and inorganic particles of matter will make water look cloudy, smell bad, and taste awful. They can clog aerators and foul solenoids in dishwashers and washing machines. They cause premature wear to kitchen and bath faucets. The particles can also make toilet flush valves and sensitive shower control valves perform erratically. Have your water tested. A water treatment company can present options on how to deal with water-quality problems. When you go to replace an aerator, always bring the old aerator to the hardware store to match it against a new one. They are available in different sizes and male/female thread configurations.

> You've got three options to deal with a plugged aerator: Brush off its screen, replace its screen, or replace the entire part.

The Sink Stinks

The sink trap is probably dry. Normally it's filled with water, a simple and effective barrier to odors from the building's plumbing or the sewer system. But if the drain system has been badly designed or poorly installed, or the vent stack on the roof is plugged with leaves and sticks, the result is the same: Draining water creates a vacuum and sucks the trap dry. Another stink source may be the sink's overflow hole. The interior cavity leading from the overflow to the drain can become black with nasty-smelling slime. Getting the drain to work properly may involve replumbing it and the vent system, but the remedy could also be as simple as clearing the vent stack with a length of wire or a plumber's snake. To make slime disappear from the overflow channel, flush it out with a cleaner that contains bleach or a mildew killer.

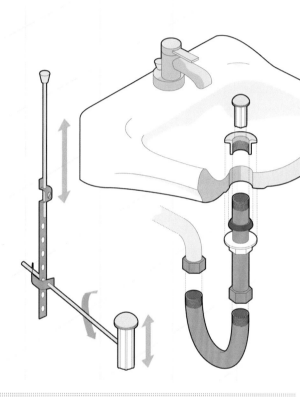

AN OLD DRAIN

First, spray a penetrating lubricant on every threaded joint in the drain assembly. Let the lubricant work for an hour or two before beginning the removal process. Start by removing the coupling nuts **(1)** that hold the trap in place, then remove the trap. Next, disconnect and remove the pop-up assembly **(2)**. There are two types of pop-ups. One has a slot that engages the pivot rod. It can be removed by twisting the plug counterclockwise and lifting it out. The other type of pop-up has a more complex pivot rod assembly (shown at left). To remove this type, squeeze the ends of the spring clip together and slide it back on the pivot rod, flexing the clevis strap back as you do so. Now unscrew the cap that holds the pivot rod assembly to the tailpiece, and remove the rod and pop-up. Next, use tongue-and-groove pliers to remove the jamb nut **(3)**. Remove the gasket above the nut, unthread the tailpiece **(4)** from the flange **(5)**, place a wood block below the flange, and tap it out with a hammer. Remember to line the bottom of the new flange with plumber's putty before pressing it into place, and use Teflon tape or pipe-joint compound on the new parts you install.

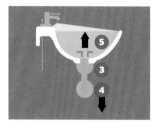

KNOW
—YOUR—
STUFF

Adhesives

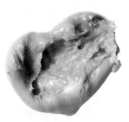   

A / CONSTRUCTION ADHESIVE

What it is: A blend of elastomers* and resins with water or solvent (or a polyurethane blend with limestone). It's usually extruded out of a tube, though trowel-grade types, which have a longer open or working time, are available in buckets for covering large areas. Materials such as clay and limestone are added to strengthen it and improve its cling to vertical or overhead surfaces.

Best for: Specific— usually big—jobs and materials, such as fastening plywood to floor joists or paneling to drywall. Clamping pressure (also called fixturing) is supplied by the weight of the workpiece or by driving a fastener through the joint between the pieces.

B / EPOXY

What it is: A two-part adhesive consisting of a resin and a curing agent. Its consistency can range from a liquid, to a gel, to a putty stick that is kneaded to mix the inner and outer layers (resin and curing agent).

Best for: Unusual bonding and repair jobs when the joint does not fit tightly or when a portion of the repaired area needs to be rebuilt with the epoxy itself. Also good for filling holes and cracks. Specific formulas bond and rebuild wood, metal, and fiberglass. Epoxies have excellent heat resistance and high strength but can be brittle in cold temperatures. Some cure under water or on wet surfaces. No clamping pressure or only light pressure is required.

C / CYANOACRYLATE

What it is: A single-component adhesive that cures quickly in the absence of air and requires a small amount of moisture in the material to be fastened. Sometimes referred to as "super glue." Its consistency can be quite thin, though modified types can flex for gap filling or enable the adhesive to cling to vertical surfaces.

Best for: Making a rapid bond when the glued parts are brought together with just hand pressure. Good for porcelain, glass, and some rigid plastics. Thin formulas are handy when you need a thin joint line (repairing broken porcelain). Thicker gel types are useful where gap filling is required. Will not work on joints thicker than 20 to 30 thousandths of an inch or on polyethylene or polypropylene.

D / POLYURETHANE GLUE

What it is: Urethane polymer and catalyst blend that requires moisture to cure. The moisture can come from the surfaces being bonded or from the air.

Best for: Joining wood to wood when a water-proof joint is required. However, it can be used to join almost all common building materials. Urethane wood glues expand as they cure, foaming slightly in the process. Keeping the joint stable during curing requires evenly distributed clamping pressure. Urethane construction adhesives do not foam but cure much more slowly than comparable products.

*ELASTOMER: a substance capable of returning to its original size after being stretched

ASK ROY

POPULAR MECHANICS' SENIOR HOME EDITOR SOLVES YOUR MOST PRESSING PROBLEMS.

(Q)

I hate caulking. Maybe it's me, but I've tried caulk-smoothing tools and masking tape, and it still comes out sort of sloppy and half-baked-looking. Even my kids commented on the sink I caulked. There has to be a better way. Help me out here.

Clean caulking comes down to three things: the position of the caulk gun, the speed at which you move it, and the opening that you cut in the end of the tube. Sure, gadgets may improve the process, but caulking is a simple DIY skill. Once you learn how to do it, it's easy and predictable without the use of additional devices. It's also a fact that caulk is overused today. It's not a building material. It's often used to fill gaps and make up for sloppy workmanship, but no matter what you do, it will always look lousy when applied in those circumstances. And while I'm on this soapbox, another culprit is the $1.99 caulk gun. Stepping up to a pro-level gun that costs just $5 makes a world of difference in getting caulk to look neat. The pressure you produce with a pro-quality gun is consistent and its pump action is predictable and much smoother.

So let's start with the tube. Cut its tip at about a 45-degree angle. Use a utility knife with a fresh blade in it, or use a 1-inch-wide, razor-sharp chisel. The nozzle tip may have lines marked into it to indicate where to cut it. In almost all cases, I find the caulk extrudes more neatly if the tube open-ing is cut closer to the tip than the manufacturer recommends. A smaller bead is neater and there's simply less material to strike off if you need to clean up the joint with your index finger.

If the bead of caulk is too small, you can always cut a little bit more off the nozzle tip. If a slight burr remains on the nozzle after you cut it, remove it by carefully paring with the knife. Next, hold the caulk gun in the joint so the tube tip meets the surface at a compound 45-degree angle. As a righty, I usually brace the nozzle with my left hand and squeeze the handle gently while simultaneously drawing the gun slowly down the joint or around the surface. Don't squeeze the handle again until there's an appreciable drop-off in the caulk coming out of the nozzle. Get the timing and pressure right and you can produce long, smooth runs with a single pump of the handle. Except when starting to run a bead in a corner, I often place the tip of my index finger over the joint. With a little downward pressure, my fingertip smooths the caulk as it comes out. The result is a nice smooth bead that doesn't need further wiping.

▶ If the joint needs extra wiping to look good, draw a moistened finger down it (assuming you're using a latex or latex blend). If you're using a caulk that requires cleanup with mineral spirits, wear a disposable nitrile glove. The glove reduces the wear and tear on your finger and will make cleanup easier when you're done. Peel the glove. Toss it out.

CAULK GUN

THE **ESSENTIAL** TOOL

Cheap caulk guns tend to extrude a messy bead. Buy a pro gun for a few dollars more. It provides consistent pressure and better feedback.

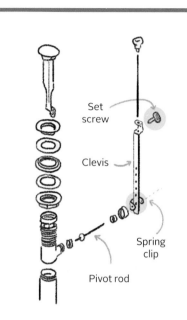

Set screw

Clevis

Spring clip

Pivot rod

Broken Pop-Up Stopper

It's not unusual to pull too hard on the lift rod of a bathroom sink—the thing that pulls down the drain plug—and find yourself holding it in your hand, plug stuck down for good. As an adult, you should be embarrassed if you have to call a plumber to fix this. In most sinks, the lift rod is connected to the drain plug by a mechanical complex that includes a clevis and a pivot rod (see diagram). In some cases the lift rod has been pulled off the set screw, which connects it to the clevis. To fix this, just put the rod back on the screw and tighten. In other cases, the clevis has slipped off the pivot rod. If you can find the spring clip, slide it onto the pivot rod, wrap it around the clevis, and then slide the other end onto the pivot rod to secure.

CLOGGED DRAIN

Fixing a clog depends on two main things: what's causing the clog, and what kind of drain the clog occurs in.

GRID DRAIN

To get hair and scum clogs out of a grid drain, remove the grid screw. Clean the screw threads and the mount bar using needle-nose pliers, a bent wire, and old scissors.

POP-UP DRAIN

Lift and tilt the stopper, and the angled hinges will slip free. Use pliers to clean the stopper and the spring within the drain.

LIFT-AND-TURN DRAIN

Remove the knurled knob from the stopper's top and undo the screw beneath. Use pliers and scissors to get hair off the mount bar in the drain.

▶ If none of those approaches work, buy yourself a hand snake and combination plunger. It shouldn't run you more than $30. First, try the plunger. Fold in the rubber cup on its front (it's used for unplugging toilets). Run water into the shower to seal around the plunger, then force its handle toward the drain and jerk it back to create a sucking action. No luck? Try the hand snake. Loosen the thumb screw and feed out about 10 inches of the coiled spring (the snake). Set the thumbscrew and crank the handle clockwise. Now pull the snake back, crank forward, and repeat until you break through. Wipe the snake clean as you crank it back into the body. Finally, run hot water down the drain to flush it clear. If you advance 10 feet of the snake and still haven't broken through, call in a pro.

POPULAR MECHANICS' SENIOR HOME EDITOR SOLVES YOUR MOST PRESSING PROBLEMS.

We have a long ranch house and it takes forever to get warm water to the farthest bathroom. Is there anything we can do?

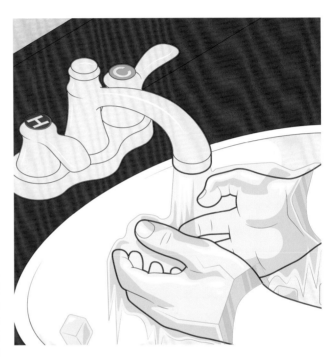

A You need a hot-water recirculation system. Instead of water moving in only one direction, from the water heater to the bathroom, it also moves cooled water from the bathroom to the water heater, making room for new hot water to take its place. A recirculation valve is installed under the bathroom sink and a circulator with a timer is installed at the water heater. The timer kicks the circulator on, and it pushes hot water up to the fixture. The recirculation valve under the sink opens and the warm water flows into the cold-water line and, eventually, back to the water heater. Of course, this occasionally results in some lukewarm water in the cold-water line, but it's better than freezing your hands. The most robust versions of this system that I've seen are the ones made by Taco. The company's Hot-Link setup even has an easy-to-clean, removable O-ring-sealed cover on the crossover valve under the sink. You could also install a tankless hot-water system with a dedicated recirculation line. Rinnai makes a small, wall-mounted, instantaneous gas water heater that supplies hot water on demand. The water can be recirculated one of three ways: periodically throughout the day, timed to align with events such as morning showers, or whenever the hot water falls below a given temperature.

KITCHEN

CHAPTER 02

ASK ROY

POPULAR MECHANICS' SENIOR HOME EDITOR SOLVES YOUR MOST PRESSING PROBLEMS.

Q **Our garbage disposal stinks. I've tried quite a few cleaning products, but nothing works. Any ideas?**

A Try my home remedy. There was an onion odor emanating from the disposal in my home, so I cut a lemon into eight wedges and put them into the appliance. I then turned on the water and let the disposal grind up the lemon. I was pleasantly surprised when this removed the odor.

If that technique doesn't work, try Disposer Care, a blue powder that you pour down the drain. When you turn on the water and the garbage disposal, the powder is converted into a foaming cleaner that scrubs away food, grease, and odors. A box of four costs less than $10 at repairclinic.com.

STUCK DISPOSAL

"Ninety-five percent of garbage disposals have a reset button on the motor," says Chris Hall, a former appliance repairman and founder of repairclinic.com. "No other appliance has this, so people assume they need to call a technician. I've answered literally dozens of calls that just needed someone to hit the reset." The button is small, usually red or black, and located on the bottom of the disposal unit under the sink.

FAULTY SINK SPRAYER

The first step in diagnosing any spray attachment on a kitchen faucet is to look beneath the sink to see if the hose is kinked. If it is, and the kink can't be corrected, replace the hose. Make sure you get either an identical replacement or one with an adapter to fit your faucet. If the hose is okay, remove the sprayer head nozzle and clean it, if necessary. The nozzle is usually screwed into the spray head. With the nozzle off, flush the spray head. If you still have a problem, then it's time to check the diverter valve.

First, remove the faucet spout. The valve can then be lifted or screwed out and cleaned. The diverter area in the faucet body should be flushed at this time by slowly opening one of the faucet handles. If the problem is not corrected after you reinstall the diverter valve, the valve is defective and should be replaced.

THE ESSENTIAL TOOL

ADJUSTABLE WRENCH

For portability and convenience, you can't beat the time-honored adjustable wrench, which enables you to turn a wide range of nuts and bolts with a single tool. If you're going to own just one, make it a 10- or 14-inch model so that it's big enough for residential plumbing fittings. Pull it so the reaction force is applied to the fixed jaw, not the movable one.

FAULTY DISHWASHER

If your dishwasher seems to run perfectly yet leaves your dishes dirty, there may be a simple fix. Open the dishwasher and remove the lower tray to access the spray arms. Gently clean the holes at the ends of the arms with a steel skewer or an awl. Don't use a wooden or plastic instrument that might break and get stuck in a hole.

Screws

The Rules

When it comes to screws, simpler is better. Where possible, use a screw with an exposed head, as opposed to a recessed head that requires an extra drilling step.

When in doubt, use a longer screw. The extra length can help make up for a less-than-perfect pilot hole and boost grip.

Invest in a set of properly sized screwdriving bits. The right bit is more likely to drive the screw and less likely to strip its head.

A / DRYWALL-TO-METAL
What it does: Attaches drywall to metal studs
How to use it: Buy "fine thread" or "metal stud" screws long enough to penetrate the drywall and dig ⅜ inch into the stud.

B / DRYWALL-TO-WOOD
What it does: Attaches drywall to wood studs
How to use it: In the store, look for the thread type printed on the box. Buy "coarse thread" screws long enough to go through the drywall, at least ⅝ inch into the stud.

C / TRADITIONAL WOOD
What it does: Joins wood parts in furniture and fastens hinges to wood
How to use it: Bore a pilot hole with a tapered or multidiameter bit. In most cases, you want a screw long enough to bury two-thirds of its length in the base lumber.

D / SELF-DRILLING
What it does: Holds thick sheet steel assemblies or sheet steel to tubing
How to use it: Drive it with a cordless drill driver and a socket bit. The screw's tip bores the hole. Select a fastener with a tip that's longer than the combined thickness of materials.

E / CONCRETE
What it does: Fastens wood or metal to concrete, brick, or mortar joints
How to use it: Bore the pilot hole ¼ inch deeper than the length of the embedded fastener. Blow dust and chips out of the hole with compressed air before inserting the screw.

F / MODERN WOOD
What it does: Fastens wood to wood and wood to composite materials
How to use it: Make a simple, single-diameter pilot hole. The screw's tip, known as a Type 17, cuts aggressively. For hardwoods, use a Dri-lube screw. The lubricant reduces torque.

G / LAG
What it does: Joins hardware to construction lumber or lumber to lumber
How to use it: Choose a lagscrew that will go into the base lumber 7 to 10 times as deep as the shank is wide. Local building codes may detail spacing and other specs.

H / SHEET-METAL
What it does: Fastens light-gauge sheet steel assemblies or small plastic parts
How to use it: Choose a hexhead screw and drive with a socket bit for maximum installation speed. Size the screw to be slightly longer than the combined thickness of the pieces.

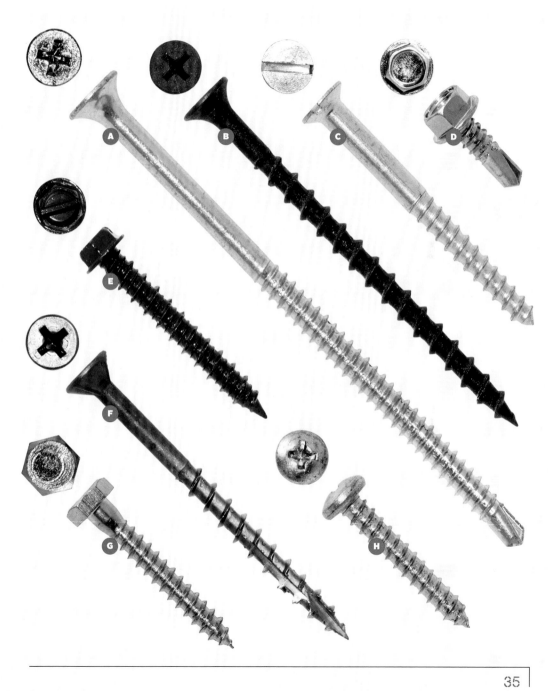

FIXING PROBLEM DRAWERS

Of all the places we find to store things, the humble drawer must be the most underappreciated and overworked accessory in our busy homes. After all, you find drawers everywhere—from kitchen to bathroom to shop. They hold the things you use every day—as well as the stuff you'd just as soon forget but can't seem to throw away.

Drawers are more than just boxes that keep your life organized. They're sliding compartments that keep things hidden and tidy. And herein lies the catch. Like anything else that moves and carries a load, drawers can wear out and parts can become loose or misaligned, making operation difficult if not impossible. And, problems occur that much sooner if the drawer was poorly made in the first place. Whatever the cause, though, making things right is easier than you might think. And in most cases, all you need is a screwdriver or two to get the job done.

While you'll find many types of drawers throughout your home, including those that run on metal slides and traditional all-wooden versions, most can be fixed using basic repair techniques. The first step is to see if your problem drawer has slides and what type of slide is used. The most common are side-mounted units. These are either heavy-duty, full-extension, ball-bearing slides used in demanding applications and hit-end cabinetry, or lighter, low-profile slides designed for light-duty use that allow for about three-fourths of the drawer to be accessible when opened.

SLIDE REPAIR

Although heavy-duty, full-extension drawer slides are very reliable, they aren't immune to problems. If you have a drawer equipped with this type of slide that sticks or doesn't slide smoothly, first remove the drawer and check for loose screws and rough or stuck ball bearings. Pull the drawer all the way out of the cabinet and locate the plastic or metal clips that hold the drawer rails to the cabinet slides. Press the clips **(1)** to release the drawer,

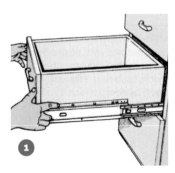

To release a drawer with full-extension slides, pull it out of the opening and then press the clip on each side.

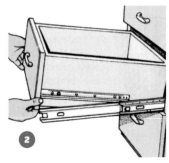

Lift the front of the drawer to free the rail from the clip. Then, pull the drawer and remove it from the slide.

then lift the front (**2**) and pull it farther out of the case to disengage it.

Examine the screws that hold the slides to the cabinet and tighten any that may have worked loose. Sometimes oiling the ball bearings with a bit of spray lubricant can help eliminate roughness, but don't expect this to do much, as they're designed to be maintenance-free.

If these steps don't solve your problem, you'll need to replace the slides. Locate the screws through the access holes and remove them (**3**). Then, remove the screws that hold the drawer rails to the sides of the drawer (**4**). The manufacturer and model number should be visible on the slide. Next, measure the length of the slide. Your repair will be easier if you get an exact replacement. If your hardware store or mail-order supplier doesn't carry the model, contact the manufacturer to locate the nearest retail outlet.

Install the new heavy-duty slides by reversing the removal procedure. Secure the new slides using the same mounting holes so that the drawer will be properly aligned. Pull the cabinet members completely out of the case to insert the drawer. Engage the back ends of the drawer rails under the catches on the sides, and then lower the front of the drawer until you hear the rails click into place.

Light-duty slides, by comparison, have two rollers on each slide of the drawer. One roller is

> ## LOOSE DRAWER KNOBS
>
> When a wooden knob comes loose from a door or drawer because the screwhole is stripped, remove the knob and stuff the screwhole with toothpicks and glue. Use a utility knife to trim the toothpicks flush. Then, replace the knob—you don't have to wait for the glue to dry—and carefully tighten the screw.

To remove the cabinet member of a full-extension slide, locate the screw through the access holes in the side.

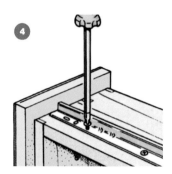

Remove a full-extension drawer rail by withdrawing the mounting screws. Use the same screw holes for the reinstallation.

With light-duty slides, pull the drawer as far as it will go. Lift the front until the rear rollers clear the stops on the slides.

mounted to the cabinet member of the slide, and one roller is found at the back of the drawer member. With such a simple mechanism, the problems that can arise are few. Either a screw can work loose and obstruct the operation of a roller, or the rollers can wear out.

To inspect the slides, first remove the drawer from the cabinet. Pull the drawer straight out until it stops, and then lift the front of the drawer until the rear rollers clear the stops on the slides **(5)**. Keep the drawer tilted up while you pull it free from the cabinet **(6)**.

Check to see that all mountain screws are tight and that their heads do not protrude into the path of the rollers. If the screws are not the problem, you should replace the slides. Remove the screws that hold the slides to the cabinet sides **(7)** and also those that hold the drawer members to the drawer **(8)**. Some slides have the screws driven into the sides of the drawer box and some have them driven in the bottom edge. Note the man-

ufacturer, model, and length of the slides and try to get an exact replacement. Install the new slides with the provided screws and check for smooth operation.

TRADITIONAL DRAWERS

In the simplest type of drawer you won't find metal slides between drawer and case. Antiques, fine handcrafted furniture, and traditional cabinetwork typically have wood drawers that ride directly within a wood enclosure. Instead of ball bearings, wood surfaces slide against each other. When these drawers stick, the cause is usually a lack of lubrication between the contacting wooden parts. In most cases, this can be remedied by applying a light coat of paste wax to the wood-to-wood contact surfaces to both the drawer and the inside of the cabinet. After applying the wax, buff it lightly. If your drawer is simply too tight, locate the area where it sticks and carefully trim with a sharp hand plane.

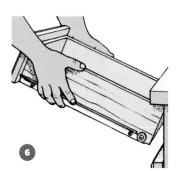

With the rear rollers free of the cabinet slides, keep the drawer tilted while you pull it free from the cabinet.

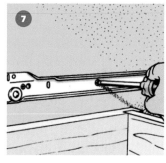

Remove the small mounting screws from the cabinet side to free a light-duty slide from the cabinet.

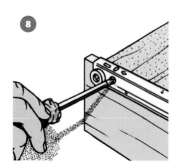

To remove the drawer component of a light-duty slide, unthread the screws that secure it to the drawer side.

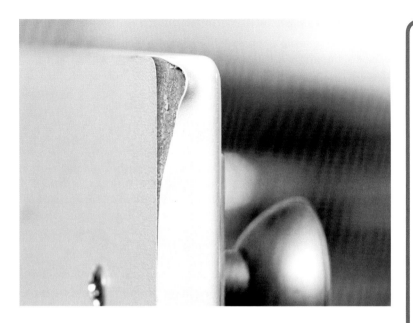

PEELING LAMINATE ON CABINET DOORS

Have a careful look at the corner of the door where the laminate is peeling up. If the core of the door appears to be sound, then the repair is simple. Use a fine-tooth hacksaw blade or a putty knife to spread some moisture-resistant adhesive under the laminate. Then, use masking tape wrapped from the front of the door and around the edge to pull the laminate down. Remove the tape once the adhesive has set, and use a razor-sharp chisel to pare off globs of adhesive that squeeze out from under the laminate while they are still soft.

On the other hand, if moisture from cooking or cleaning has caused the core of the doors to crumble or otherwise fail, you're better off replacing those doors or replacing all the doors in the kitchen. You will find it very difficult to make the laminate adhere properly to a deteriorated substrate.

Kitchen cabinet doors can be ordered at some lumberyards and home centers and on the web through sites such as cabinetdoordepot.com.

LOOSE BACKSPLASH TILES

Many kitchen backsplashes are glued to the wall. Over time, they can pull free, exposing the wall behind the counter to water damage. To reattach a loose backsplash, first use a putty knife to scrape off any old glue. Apply two beads of construction adhesive to the rear of the backsplash tiles and a bead of clear silicone sealant along the tiles' bottom edge. Set the backsplash in position and press it against the wall and counter. To hold the backsplash while the adhesive cures, wedge 1 × 2 strips diagonally between the top edge of the backsplash and the underside of the upper kitchen wall cabinet.

YOUR FRIDGE LEAKS

The common culprit is an icemaker line, which can spring leaks. If you can't repair the line right away, there is a shutoff valve. Typically, it's under the sink. If not, look in the basement, beneath the fridge.

WALLS, CEILINGS & FLOORS

CHAPTER

HOLES IN DRYWALL

First, cut a neat drywall patch (1). Make it generously oversize. Hold it over the hole and trace neatly around the patch with a sharp pencil. Take a drywall saw and cut on the outside of the pencil line **(2)**. Now take the patch, drive two drywall screws into it to serve as handles and test-fit it in the hole. If the patch doesn't fit, here's a down-and-dirty trick: Put your thumb about midway behind the blade of the saw and scrape its teeth sideways over the patch's high spot. The coarse teeth plane down the edge of the drywall. If the ridges left by the teeth need to be shaved off, flip the saw over and do the same move with the back of the saw.

Finally, butter the edge of the patch like it was a brick, and simply set it into the hole **(3)**. Wipe off excess drywall compound with a 6-inch knife, but don't bother being too fussy. After the compound is dry, sand the repair smooth. Apply compound as needed to blend it into the surrounding surface. You can often skip the drywall tape on most repairs and not have a problem. But tape a really big repair—say, a patch that is 1 foot square. Drywall tape is even more important for a durable repair if the patch is located in a zone that could see additional abuse, such as where a doorknob may strike.

▶ With modifications, the same procedure can be used on ceilings. Use a strip of drywall inserted into the ceiling cavity and screwed to the patch. This acts as a brace that holds the repair up while the drywall compound hardens.

FOR SMALL HOLES IN A WALL

Simply slap on a peel-and-stick drywall patch. You can also use a method in which you cut out the patch but carve away the drywall around the perimeter so the patch's paper forms a flange. Put the patch in the hole and apply compound over the paper flange.

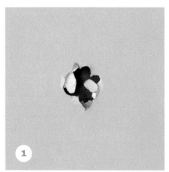

Cut a neat, generously oversize patch and trace around it.

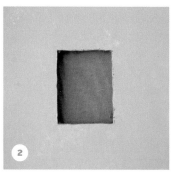

Using a drywall saw, cut on the outside of the line.

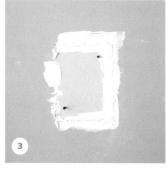

Drive in two drywall screw "handles," apply compound to the patch edges, and insert it.

Painter's Knives

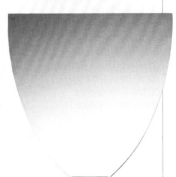

A / CHISEL-EDGE/ PUTTY KNIFE

Best for: Scraping loose paint, lifting small pieces of wallpaper, removing crumbling window putty, decal removal

Details: Tool has a thick ($5/64$-inch) high-carbon-steel blade with an edge ground to a chisel-shaped bevel.

B / FLEXIBLE 4-INCH KNIFE

Best for: Spreading drywall compound, patching cracks, light scraping

Details: Blade is $1/32$-inch-thick high-carbon steel. Better models are more abuse-tolerant; they are constructed so that the blade tang runs the length of the handle.

C / PAINTER'S TOOL

Best for: Cleaning excess paint off rollers, scraping paint and raking failed caulk out of siding and trim or weeds from sidewalk control joints

Details: A jack-of-all-trades tool with a $5/64$-inch-thick blade. Some models have a metal cap on the end of the handle for bumping in loose drywall nails.

D / DISPOSABLE KNIFE

Best for: Touching up putty or drywall compound on painted surfaces without leaving scuff marks

Details: Blade is made from flexible polystyrene. Bending it after putty or filler has dried is often enough to crack off and remove hardened goo, prolonging the tool's use.

ASK ROY

POPULAR MECHANICS' SENIOR HOME EDITOR SOLVES YOUR MOST PRESSING PROBLEMS.

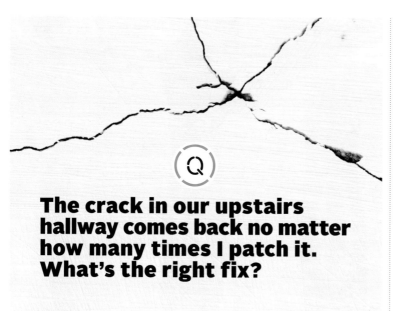

Ⓠ

The crack in our upstairs hallway comes back no matter how many times I patch it. What's the right fix?

Ⓐ Seasonal cracks in drywall and plaster are tough to repair. As they open and close, one of two things happens: The surface around the crack crushes and grinds the patch material or it pulls it apart, ripping the material away from the wall or ceiling surface. You need a super-flexible material and one that can bridge a wide gap. I've used DAP ElastoPatch with good results. The material is about the consistency of yogurt, and you can apply it with a 6-inch putty knife. Although it's pretty simple to use, it'll take you a few tries before you can produce a smooth finish. I'd recommend experimenting on a cast-off bit of drywall first.

Before you patch, use a painter's 5-in-1 tool to rake out the former repair materials. Then scoop out the patch and spread it on in thin layers. Wipe off any excess (you won't be able to sand it down like joint compound), let the patch dry, then paint.

Q: We just bought a new home, and the walls have a number of small bulges, shaped like fastener heads. What are these, and how can we fix them before we paint?

A: Those bulges are called nail pops. They're created when drying lumber pulls away from the nail or screw used to hold the drywall in place. The fastener's head sticks in the drywall instead of pulling away with the lumber, which creates a telltale bump.

To fix yours, use a 5-in-1 tool to scrape the drywall off the fastener's head. You've seen this tool before: It looks like a putty knife with a hook-shaped blade. If what you find below is a screw, try backing it out. If you can't get it, leave it. If you find a nail, set it a little deeper.

Next, drive an 1¼-inch drywall screw above and below the nail pop. Apply a couple of coats of drywall compound. Now you can repaint.

our receipt
M SelfCheck™ System

ems that you checked out

itle: Catastrophic care : how American
      health care killed my father--and how
      we can fix it / David Goldhil
ue: Tuesday, March 31, 2020

itle: How to fix anything : essential home
      repairs anyone can do.
ue: Tuesday, March 31, 2020

itle: Meditation for fidgety skeptics : a 10%
      happier how-to book / Dan Harris and
      Jeff Warren with Carlye
ue: Tuesday, March 31, 2020

itle: Superfood soups : 100 delicious,
      energizing & plant-based recipes / Julie
      Morris ; [photography by O
ue: Tuesday, March 31, 2020

itle: The plot against the president : the true
      story of how Congressman Devin
      Nunes uncovered the biggest
ue: Tuesday, March 31, 2020

itle: The power of full engagement :
      [managing energy, not time, is the key
      to high performance and person
ue: Tuesday, March 31, 2020

otal items: 6
/10/2020 2:45 PM

hank you for using the
Glastonbury Library.

Q The ceiling fan in my master bedroom is awfully wobbly. How can I make it true?

A Assuming the fan was properly installed, it could be out of balance; this can be corrected with a fan blade balancing kit sold at a home center. They cost about $5. More ominously, the fan may have been hung in an electrical box that wasn't rated to support it, or it could have loosened for a variety of other reasons: Its mounting screws may have missed the joist, for instance. This is more than an annoyance. I know of one case in which a ceiling fan fell and struck a woman sleeping in the bed below. She's lucky she wasn't hurt. For now, stop using the fan. Then either refasten the box to the framing or overhaul the entire setup with a new box rated to support the fan.

DUSTING CEILING FAN BLADES

Fan blades are dust magnets, and cleaning them is a hassle. Half the dust you wipe off the blades ends up in your face. Swap the feather duster for a pillowcase. Slip the pillowcase over the fan blade, and as you wipe off the dust it stays contained.

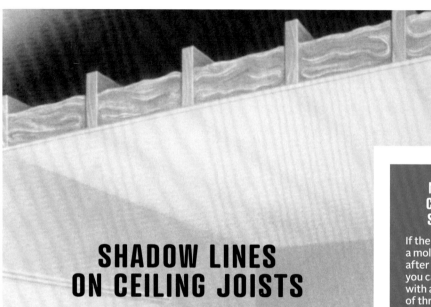

SHADOW LINES
ON CEILING JOISTS

Dark lines on the drywall ceiling below the attic are a sign of an insulation problem. Even if you have insulation between the joists in the attic floor, the tops of the joists are exposed to the low winter temperatures in the attic. Since the wood joists are not effective insulators, they act as thermal bridges. Consequently, the temperature at the underside of the joists (at the drywall ceiling) is lower than the adjacent sections of the ceiling that are covered with the insulation batts. Because of the lower temperature below the joists, condensation (however slight) tends to form along these areas. Over time, the moisture traps dust and also results in mildew growth, which shows up as shadow lines.

To prevent this from recurring, first paint the ceiling. Use a paint containing mildewcide. Next, install insulation batts over the exposed ceiling joists. Ideally, the insulation should fill the spaces between the joists and cover the tops of the joists as well. This last layer of batts is installed perpendicular to the joists. However you install the insulation, make sure to use a type that does not have a foil or kraft-paper vapor barrier. And be sure additional insulation does not cover soffit vents or recessed light housings (unless the housings are IC types rated for direct contact with insulation).

MOLDY CEILING STAINS

If the ceiling has a mold buildup after a leak, you can clean it with a solution of three parts water to one part bleach. Dab it on the ceiling, and wait 20 minutes before rinsing it off. Blot the area dry with a paper towel. However, once you remove the mold, you may find that a pale brown stain remains on the ceiling. You can't simply paint over the stain. After a few months, the stain will bleed through the paint. To be sure that the stain does not resurface, apply a primer sealer before painting.

Fillers

A / SPACKLING PASTE
Best for: Filling small cracks and minor dents in wood, masonry, and metal
Details: Formulated for specific jobs, such as interior or exterior work, or shallow dents, such as those in metal doors

B / COLORED WOOD PUTTY
Best for: Concealing nail holes and minor surface blemishes
Details: A soft putty that retains its flexibility. Buy several shades and blend to make a perfect color match.

C / EPOXY STICK
Best for: Odd jobs, repairing metal, or resetting hardware on knockdown furniture
Details: Inner and outer portions of the stick must be mixed thoroughly and used quickly before the mixed portion hardens.

D / EPOXY-BASED WOOD FILLER
Best for: Rebuilding primed wood architectural elements, such as windowsills
Details: Carve off excess before it hardens to reduce the need for excessive sanding or grinding.

SQUEAKY WOOD FLOORS

Hardwood and carpeted floors squeak when the subfloor below flexes down against the floor joist. The Squeeeeek No More kit fastens the loose subfloor to the joist. Its **floor fixture (1)** positions and snaps off screws driven through hardwood floors. The **screws (2)** have a square drivehead and a scored shank to help them break off cleanly below the floor's surface. The **alignment tool (3)** assists in driving screws into carpeted floors; a notch in its side

helps you grab the screwhead and cleanly snap it and part of the shank below the surface of the subfloor. The **specialty drive bit (4)** has a stop collar formed in its shank; it's used with both the hardwood-floor fixture and the alignment tool for carpeted floors. Two **square-drive joist-finding bits (5)** are included with every kit. Drive one at each end of a joist to form a sightline to help you keep the screws on track as you work down the length of the joist.

ANOTHER EASY FIX

If the space underneath the floor is accessible, locate the squeak from below by having someone walk across the floor. Once you've pinpointed the spot, spread glue on both sides of a thin wooden shim, and tap it into the space between the floor joist and the plywood subfloor. Be careful not to drive the shim in too far; you don't want to raise the floor. The goal is to fill any voids that allow movement.

BOUNCING FLOORS

You can usually eliminate springiness by nailing "sister" joists of the same size to every other existing joist. When installing these joists, you may need to notch or shave the ends so they fit between the subfloor and the sill. Although it's typically unnecessary, you can always add more sister joists to the remaining joists to stiffen the floor further.

INDENTATIONS IN THE CARPET

You can often remove carpet indentations caused by furniture with a steam iron. To do this, hold an iron over the depression and apply steam to it. Don't press the iron down on the spot. Saturate the area with steam, then rake the fibers with your fingers. Depending on how old and deep the depression is, it may be necessary to steam the area several times to remove it.

10 Litre ℮

YOU DON'T WANT YOUR PAINT ROLLER TO DRY OUT

If you have to pause a painting job, wrap your roller and brushes tightly in a plastic bag and stick them in the freezer. Once thawed, they'll be ready to use. Just be sure to seal the bag tightly to eliminate any chance of food contamination.

FIXING DOOR PROBLEMS

Like most things mechanical, doors can develop problems. Fortunately, fixing a problem door doesn't require years of experience or special training. In fact, a homeowner can handle most jobs with just a few simple hand tools and a bit of patience.

Although many problems are the result of ordinary wear and tear, some seem to appear on their own. For example, doors can be affected by the settling of a house—a common occurrence over time. The causes can be many, but the most likely are an improperly prepared foundation or drying and shrinking framing lumber. In some situations, settling can be caused by floor joists sagging under the load of a roomful of furniture.

STICKY FIXES

One of the most common signs of structural settling is doors that stick when they are closed. Most often, the problem is seen in a door that has started to rub against the top of the head jamb. You might notice that the paint on the jamb is beginning to wear at a particular spot.

Since rebuilding the door jambs to make them square is a major undertaking, the most straightforward approach is to trim the door to fit the opening. Begin by marking the spot on the door where it is sticking. Next, remove the pins on the door hinge to free the door. You may have to use an old screwdriver and hammer to drive out the pins **(1)**. Remove the door and lay it flat on a pair of sawhorses or a worktable. Then, use a sharp block plane to trim the door in the area that you marked **(2)**. To keep from splitting the wood at the door edges, be sure to plane in from each edge toward the center. Don't remove too much material at first. Hang the door and test its operation. Repeat the procedure if necessary until the door operates without binding. Once it shuts properly, prime and paint the trimmed surface to seal it against moisture.

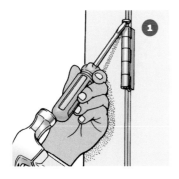

To free the door, remove the hinge pins. If the pins are tight, use an old screwdriver and a hammer to drive them out.

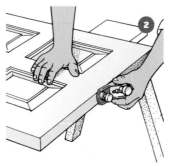

With the door on sawhorses, use a sharp plane to take light cuts. Work from each edge toward the center.

SLOPPY HINGES

Heavily used doors often have problems at the hinges. If you

THE
ESSENTIAL
TOOL

LOCKING PLIERS

An early multitool, locking pliers—patented in 1924—are sometimes known by the brand name Vise-grip. They function like ordinary pliers but also as a wrench or welding clamp. Their powerful grip works well to remove stubborn nails or fence staples.

have a door that rubs against the jamb on its lock edge, a loose hinge is the most probable cause. To fix it, first try tightening the hinge screws **(3)**. Select the proper-size screwdriver to avoid stripping the slot in the screwhead, then firmly tighten the screws in both the jamb and door.

If the hinges have been loose for some time, or if you've tightened them several times already and the problem persists, it is likely that the screwholes have become worn or stripped. In this case, replace the original screws with ones that are about 1 inch longer and of the same number size. First, remove the existing screws and bore small-diameter pilot holes for the new screws directly through the old holes **(4)**. Then, install the longer screws.

DOORSTOP REPAIR

Occasionally, a door will develop problems with the stop—especially the stop on the latch edge of the door. If this is the case, you'll notice a gap between the face of the door and the stop when the door is fully closed and the latch is engaged.

In some instances, the stop can prevent the latch from working. Most likely, the cause is a door that has warped. While a properly constructed door shouldn't warp excessively, most doors warp a little over time. Environments that allow for different temperature and humidity conditions on opposite sides of the door are the usual causes. Bathroom, basement, and garage doors are prime examples. Also, different finishes applied to opposite faces of a door can invite warping.

Attempting to flatten a warped door is a difficult, and often impossible, job. You can, however, adjust the stops on the frame to accommodate the warp in the door. Provided the problem isn't severe, this is the simplest solution.

Since the door is fixed against the hinge jamb, any problems with the stops usually occur on the opposite side. Use a small, flat pry bar to loosen the stop on that side. Begin at the bottom end and gradually work your way to the top **(5)**.

Next, look for any nails that may remain in the jamb, and pull them out with a claw hammer.

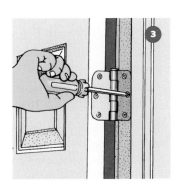
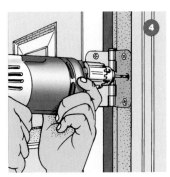

If a hinge is loose, first try tightening the screws. If the holes are worn and the screws won't hold, install longer screws.

Before installing longer screws, bore deeper pilot holes using the existing screwholes as guides.

When the door doesn't close properly against the stop, use a pry bar to remove the stop so it can be repositioned.

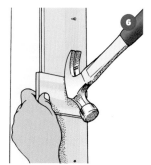

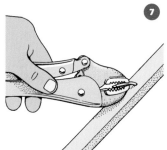

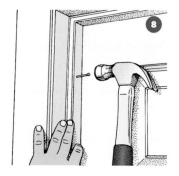

Use a claw hammer to remove nails remaining in the jamb. A wooden shim under the hammer protects the jamb.

If nails remain in the stop, pull them out of the back face with locking pliers. Don't drive them back through the front face.

To reinstall the stop, first close the door. Then, position the stop against the door and drive 3d finishing nails into the jamb.

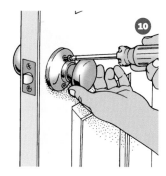

If the latch doesn't engage the hole in the strike plate, you may be able to fix it by enlarging the hole with a file.

To replace a latchset, remove screws that hold the knob in place. If there are no screws, look for clips on the inside of the knob and rose.

With the screws removed, pull the knobs from each door face. Inside the hole you'll find the latch mechanism.

Use a small shim or wood pad under the hammer head so you don't damage the jamb surface **(6)**. If there are nails in the stop after it has been removed, use locking pliers to pull them out from the back side of the piece **(7)**. Do not drive the nails out with a hammer, as this may cause splintering. After pulling the nails through, you'll be left with small, clean holes that are easy to fill.

Close the door, allowing the latch to fully engage the strike plate. Examine the joint between the door and the head stop to make sure there's no gap. If a large gap exists, or if there is a problem getting the door to latch properly, remove the head stop also.

With the door latched, hold the stop that you removed in place with its edge tightly against the face of the door. Nail the stop in this position using 3d finishing nails **(8)**. Then install the head stop if you removed it. Set the nailheads and fill all the nail holes.

LATCH WORK

Occasionally, when a doorframe settles, the lock can no longer engage the strike plate. Since the strike plate is normally mortised into the jamb, moving it isn't recommended. Instead, use a small mill file to enlarge the hole in the plate so that the latch can extend fully when the door closes **(9)**. In most cases, the hole in the jamb will be big enough to accommodate the enlarged hole in the strike plate. If it isn't, simply remove the plate and widen the hole with a sharp chisel.

Sometimes, the only thing wrong is a broken

> ### SQUEAKY HINGES
>
> Remove one of the hinge pins with a hammer and a small screwdriver or nail set, then buff it smooth with 120-grit sandpaper. Be sure to sand off all rust, dried paint, and caked-on gunk. Next, spray the pin with a light coating of silicone lubricant. Tap the newly buffed pin back into place and repeat for the remaining hinge pins.

or defective latchset. Replacing a lock isn't that difficult, especially if you can find a similar model. If there is no information on the hardware, bring it to a hardware store or locksmith to find a replacement.

To replace an old latchset, first remove the screws that hold the knobs to the door **(10)**. In most cases, the screws are clearly visible on the inside rose of the lock.

If you don't see any screws, you'll have to remove the inner knob and rose. Depress the small release clip on the knob stem and pull the knob away from the door. Then, depress the clip on the rose and gently pry it away from the door.

Pull the halves of the latchset apart to remove them from the door **(11)**. Remove the screws that hold the latch to the door **(12)**, and pull the latch out of the door **(13)**. If the latch fits tightly in its mortise, you may have to gently pry it out. To install the new lock, simply reverse the removal procedure.

When diagnosing door problems, keep in mind that several conditions can exist at the same time. For example, a door that binds can stress the hinge screws and lead to loose hinges. Spend some time studying the door, looking closely as you open and close it, to locate the source of the problem. If in doubt, try the most conservative approach first.

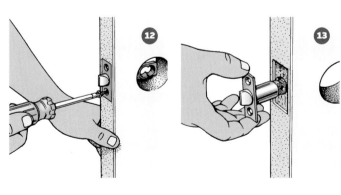

Remove the screws that hold the latch to the door. If the component is snug, gently pry at the opposite end.

Pull the assembly free. Replace it with an exact match, if possible. Reverse the procedure to install the new hardware.

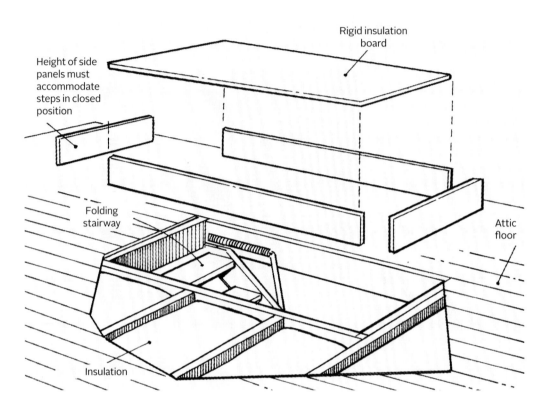

Rigid insulation board

Height of side panels must accommodate steps in closed position

Folding stairway

Attic floor

Insulation

DRAFTY FOLDING STAIRS TO THE ATTIC

This problem is quite common. An easy and effective solution is to construct a rigid insulation cover for the stairway. In addition to reducing the draft, the cover will reduce the heat loss through that area. You can use an easily available, rigid, foam-insulation board, such as Styrofoam, to construct your insulation cover. The top of the cover should be large enough to overlap the perimeter of the stairway opening by a couple of inches. The sides must be deep enough to accommodate the folding stairway in its closed position.

Once the top and four sides are cut to size, they can be attached to one another with an adhesive.

The solvent in some adhesives will react with Styrofoam. Be sure that the product you buy is compatible with the material you're gluing. A 1-inch-thick Styrofoam board has a thermal resistance (R-factor) of about 5. For greater thermal resistance, either double up on the Styrofoam or insulate the cover with fiberglass batts. Since the cover will weigh only a few pounds, it can easily be moved around when you use the stairway.

ENERGY LEAKS

ATTIC ENTRIES

Many houses have a small, uninsulated plywood or drywall hatch in the ceiling of an upstairs closet. Oftentimes, that entry goes unused because a more convenient pull-down attic entry ladder has been installed. Peel back insulation over the hatch and seal its perimeter with spray foam insulation. As to the pull-down ladder, seal the edge of its door using weatherstripping. Next, build a cover that fits over the pull-down stairs using polystyrene insulation and construction adhesive, such as Liquid Nails LN-950 Ultra Duty Poly or LN-903 Heavy Duty Construction and Remodeling adhesive. The cover must be large enough so that it fits over the folded ladder.

Caution: Watch your step in the attic. One wrong step and you'll break through the drywall ceiling—and that may not be all you break.

PIPE, DUCT, CABLE, AND VENTS

Most attics have pipe, duct, cable, and vents entering and exiting through holes drilled in wall framing and the drywall ceiling. Seal each entry using spray foam insulation.

Caution: Do not use spray foam around older recessed light fixtures that are not rated for insulation contact. It creates a fire hazard. In the long term, plan on replacing noninsulation-contact recessed lights with insulation-contact lights to prevent energy loss. Also, add a second layer of unfaced insulation to the attic if only one layer is in place.

KNEE WALL DOOR

Houses that have a finished attic often have a short wall, called a knee wall, that spans the floor and rafters. A small, uninsulated plywood door gives access to the area behind the knee wall. This may be in the room or in the back of a closet. Insulate the door's back by gluing rigid polystyrene insulation to it using a compatible construction adhesive, such as the Liquid Nails products mentioned previously.

SAGGING INSULATION

Work and storage areas in attics and garages are often insulated but unfinished. Support sagging insulation in these areas with duct tape spanning the wall, ceiling, or roof framing. Drive two staples through the tape at each framing location.

Caution: This is not a permanent fix. Drywall installed on walls and ceilings provides permanent insulation support, seals drafts, and increases fire resistance of walls and ceilings.

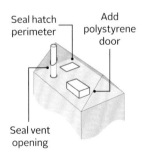

Seal hatch perimeter

Add polystyrene door

Seal vent opening

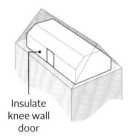

Insulate knee wall door

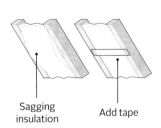

Sagging insulation

Add tape

FURNITURE & FIXTURES

CHAPTER 04

USE AN IRON TO FIX DENTED WOOD

Working with wood is often a bumpy road, and mishaps are inevitable. One of the most frustrating things that can happen in the course of a project is when a tool is dropped on a piece of carefully prepared stock, leaving an unsightly dent. After the groans and oaths have subsided, it's relatively easy to fix the problem. Place a few drops of clean water in the dent and allow it to soak in for about a minute.

Place a clean cotton cloth over the dent and use a household iron, on a medium-high setting, to heat the dent. The steam will cause the crushed wood fibers to swell, bringing the dented area flush to the surrounding material. You may have to repeat the procedure two or three times to repair a stubborn dent. The steam will raise the woodgrain, so you will need to sand the surface once the dent is gone.

NUTS TOUCH UP FURNITURE

Nicks and scratches on wood furniture with a dark finish can be easily concealed. Rub the meat of an unsalted pecan or walnut on the damaged area. The nut's oils will stain the wood.

FROM THE ARCHIVES

FILL A STRIPPED SCREWHOLE WITH A GOLF TEE

Enlarged screwholes can be quickly repaired,
we said in March 1972, by filling the
hole with a wooden golf tee. Use a hacksaw
to saw the tee flush with the wood's surface,
then sand and finish.

CROOKED PICTURES

Tired of straightening picture frames? Permanently place framed paintings or mirrors with a 12-pack of ½-inch-diameter stick-on vinyl or rubber bumpers. Affix the bumpers to the rear lower corners of every frame; their soft, antiskid rubber keeps the frames from sliding out of position.

SAGGING SHELVES

It seems every bookcase has a shelf sagging under the weight of too many volumes. A permanently bowed shelf is not only unattractive, it's potentially dangerous: If the shelf fails, it can send an avalanche of books tumbling down. Here's one solution: Support it with a vertical divider cut from ¾-inch plywood, fitted between shelves and oriented like a large book. Make the divider tall enough to prop up the shelf to its original, level height. Conceal the exposed plywood edge with a veneer edge (or, if you're feeling crafty, a tailored book jacket). To provide proper support for upper shelves and eliminate additional sagging, the lowest divider must rest on the bottom of the bookcase.

▶ An alternative: To add rigidity, glue and nail a ¾-inch-thick 1½-inch-wide piece of hardwood board to the front edge of the shelf. Then support the rear edge with a shelf peg drilled into the back of the cabinet.

DEAD OUTLET

If the lamp goes out, but the bulb's not fried, it's time to check the outlet. Once you turn off the breaker, here's how to fix the usual suspects.

DETACHED WIRE

Cut the damaged wire ⅛ inch from the end. Strip ½ inch of insulation. Reattach by bending the wire clockwise under the terminal screw, and tighten.

LOOSE PUSH-IN CONNECTION

Reattach the loose wire on the back of the outlet under the appropriate terminal screw.

LOOSE SPLICE

Remove the wire connector and replace it with a pro-quality Ideal 341 or 3M Super Tan. Hold the stripped wires so their ends are even and tighten the new connector.

TIP

To ensure that the splice is secure, gently tug on each wire.

Nail Polish Remover Removes Other Things

For spot treatment in a minor mishap—like touch-up paint that has dripped on a door hinge—acetone nail polish remover can help. Use it to dampen a rag, then hold the rag briefly against the splotch before rubbing it clean.

WOBBLY FURNITURE

When balancing a wobbly table or chair, grab a pad of Post-It notes. The ubiquitous office product is an ideal shim: It can be fine-tuned by removing individual notes, and paper won't scratch even the softest wood flooring. When in doubt, measure twice, peel once.

THE
ESSENTIAL
TOOL

WOOD CHISEL

"My favorite tool is a big, flat 10-inch chisel with a boxwood handle," woodworker Keith Fritz of Ferdinand, Indiana, says. "It's English, made in the 19th century, and has a good weight to it. That's the tool in my hand the most." Fritz grew up in the no-stoplight community of Siberia, Indiana, where both his father and grandfather farmed land and worked wood. As a high school student, he won back-to-back annual statewide competitions, one of them for an intricate Chippendale-style secretary with slots, drawers, and secret compartments. Bill and Hillary Clinton own one of his dining tables, which sell for up to $30,000. At his shop in Jasper he builds furniture inspired by old designs using mostly hand tools—and never a scrap of sandpaper. "You can tell an antique is real by looking at the tool marks," he says. "Pre-1880, there was no sanding involved. I can get the same effect with a really sharp chisel."

Chisels

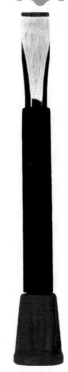

A / WOOD
How to use: Place bevel up or down and push or tap to make thin paring cuts. Place bevel up and strike firmly for aggressive shopping.
Hit: 16-ounce claw hammer is optimal for a chisel with a metal-capped handle. Use a mallet on wood-handle chisels.
Safety: Keep it razor-sharp, or it's dangerously prone to slipping.

B / METAL
How to use: Mark metal with a carbide scriber or awl, then place chisel tip in the scored line.
Hit: 16-to 32-ounce ball-peen hammer
Safety: Chisels cut medium-hard metals, not hardened steel—or heat-softened metal. (These are called "cold-chisels.") Endcaps prevent handle damage.

C / BRICK
How to use: Use a carpenter's pencil to mark the brick, then tap to score a line to prepare for a breaking hammer blow. Works with standard, refractory, or paving brick.
Hit: 16- and 24-ounce bricklayer's hammer
Safety: Don't use on concrete block or rock. For those jobs you'll need a mason's chisel or a rock chisel.

D / CONCRETE
How to use: Called a "bullpen," this tool punches through concrete block and chips away poured concrete. It's brutally efficient for demolition and requires less force than you might think.
Hit: 3-pound hand sledge
Safety: Hand-guard models are safest.

ASK ROY

POPULAR MECHANICS' SENIOR HOME EDITOR SOLVES YOUR MOST PRESSING PROBLEMS.

Every time I tighten or redrive the mounting screws on our handrail, it always comes loose again. What am I doing wrong?

A: Once a part works loose, creating an airspace between it and its mounting surface, the looseness acts as a force multiplier. You tighten it and it loosens even more. The cycle repeats until the part comes completely undone or breaks. The moral? Tighten something as soon as it comes loose; otherwise it will only get worse. When tightening, check if the threads are stripped, if anything was over- or under- tightened, or if the wrong size or type of fastener was used. There's usually a good reason that tight things become loose.

The first thing to do in your repair is ensure that the mounting screws for the brackets are hitting solid lumber. Make a test run with a $\frac{1}{16}$-inch drill bit to confirm that the screws aren't catching the edge of the stud. Next, try using a longer screw of the same diameter so it fits through the existing mounting hole but reaches a fresh part of the stud. You may be tempted to try to fix the stripped-out hole by inserting a piece of copper wire or a glue-covered golf tee, but not here. You need to reach solid lumber. If that doesn't work, you'll need a thicker and larger mounting bracket. You might even sneak in one structural screw (a hybrid fastener, somewhere between a lag screw and a wood screw) at each bracket location. Even if you have to slightly drill out the screw-mounting hole to accept the structural screw, it'd be worth it to fix this problem for good.

Q: We accidentally sanded through the top layer of wood veneer on our coffee table. What do we do?

A: The simplest solution is to hide the damage with pigmented finish like Minwax PolyShades, a combination stain and polyurethane. Each coat darkens the surface and makes the damage less visible. To apply, pour the finish out of the can and into a disposable plastic paint pot, being sure to get any thickened material off the bottom of the can. Stir the finish gently but thoroughly, then use a soft, natural-bristle brush to apply thin layers in long, slow strokes. Finish each coat by very lightly dragging the brush bristles over the fresh surface.

Let the finish dry, typically six to eight hours. Then, using No. 000 (extra-fine) or No. 0000 (finest) steel wool, go over the surface to remove any roughness and imperfections. Apply another coat. Continue until you've adequately hidden the damage.

Am I the only one who wastes all this time removing broken nails and stripped screws?

You're not alone. As the years have gone by I've become more resourceful when removing stuck or broken fasteners. The result is that I'm getting more efficient at dismantling and I'm suffering fewer skinned knuckles. By the way, a deft touch succeeds over brute force any day.

One of the best and most unusual removal tools I've found in recent years is the CoBolt from Knipex (model 71 41 200). It's a hybrid of a bolt cutter and offset diagonal cutting pliers. I use it to dig out nails, lift staples, and snip through screws, bolts, and small chain links. Forged from chrome vanadium tool steel, it can bite firmly into a hardened-steel roll pin, allowing you to lever out the offending object. The CoBolt deals with a stuck Woodruff key the same way, which is to say, effortlessly. At 8 inches it slides into your back pocket or pouch. The German-made tool is expensive but worth every penny.

On a related note, you can save time by deciding before you begin a project whether to salvage the object you plan to fix. Sometimes it's much simpler, faster, and even cheaper to cut something free and replace it than it is to coax out a fastener or pry something apart, all with the intention of reassemblage. I'm conscious of saving money and loath to send things to the landfill unnecessarily, but I'm also fairly decisive about when to fiddle with a fix or leave something at the curb.

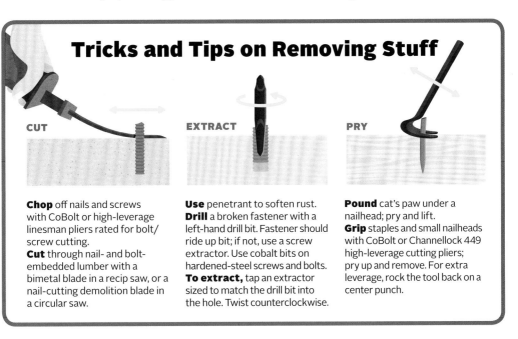

Tricks and Tips on Removing Stuff

CUT

Chop off nails and screws with CoBolt or high-leverage linesman pliers rated for bolt/screw cutting.
Cut through nail- and bolt-embedded lumber with a bimetal blade in a recip saw, or a nail-cutting demolition blade in a circular saw.

EXTRACT

Use penetrant to soften rust.
Drill a broken fastener with a left-hand drill bit. Fastener should ride up bit; if not, use a screw extractor. Use cobalt bits on hardened-steel screws and bolts.
To extract, tap an extractor sized to match the drill bit into the hole. Twist counterclockwise.

PRY

Pound cat's paw under a nailhead; pry and lift.
Grip staples and small nailheads with CoBolt or Channellock 449 high-leverage cutting pliers; pry up and remove. For extra leverage, rock the tool back on a center punch.

THE LAWS OF EXTRACTION

There are many tried-and-true tools for removing a damaged fastener, and we've all used them: the cold chisel hit with a ball-peen hammer, the cat's paw, the claw hammer, the nail puller, and the hacksaw. But sometimes even old favorites don't work. The right tool and technique mean that you, not the fastener, will prevail.

Techniques

RIP
Grab a broken, partially removed nail with a 10-inch tongue and groove pliers. Lever the tool against the curved jaw to rip the nail out of its hole. Works well on nails up to 8d.

NIP
When the access is only from above, you can cut the broken nail flush with 10-inch end-cutting pliers and then leave it in place.

CHOP
With side access to the damaged fastener, chop it flush using electrician's side-cutting pliers. Easily cuts fasteners with a diameter up to 3/16 inch.

CUT
Grip a hacksaw blade, or even a snapped-off piece of one, in locking pliers to saw off large bolts, screws, and hardware when there isn't room for the hacksaw.

Specialized Tools

Try using a **left-handed spiral bit** and running the drill in reverse. This ejects the fastener and works best when the axis of the fastener and the bit are closely aligned. Left-hand-thread drill bits are available in diameters from 5/64 to 1/2 inch.

Fit a **bolt extractor** over a damaged bolt head and back out the fastener using a 3/8- or 1/2-inch-drive ratchet. These work on bolts with heads from 1/4 to 1 inch.

Drill a **spiral-shank screw extractor** into the stripped screw first. Then lightly hammer the extractor into the hole, fit a tap wrench over the extractor's stem, and turn counterclockwise. The extractor's left-hand threads cut into the fastener.

A **multispline extractor** removes damaged socket screws, sheared-off pipe nipples, or rounded bolts. It works the same as a spiral-shank extractor, but you turn it using an open-end wrench. It works on fasteners with diameters from 1/8 to 1 11/16 inch.

To remove pipe or thin-wall tubing, press a **square-shank screw extractor** into it, then back out the extractor using a tap wrench. It works on pipe and fittings with inside diameters from 1/8 to 1 1/4 inch.

It takes a stubby drill driver or a right-angle attachment to install a pocket screw between a chair's parts. Save space by inserting the bit directly into the chuck, rather than in a magnetic bit holder.

WOBBLY CHAIRS

Glue alone won't work. It's natural to think that it would do the job. Like most homeowners, you squirted some glue into a loose joint and hoped for the best. But, unfortunately, applying a thick glob of adhesive is actually counterproductive. Wood adhesives work best when you apply a thin film of the sticky stuff to both sides of a joint, then use pressure to force the parts together. Furthermore, you almost always have to rebuild the joint, reinforce it, or disassemble it and remove adhesives from previous repairs to get it to fit properly.

Let's take a closer look at this. For a chair to be moved around easily, it has to be lightly built. Yet the loads a chair accommodates are severe. A chair may weigh 10 pounds, but it has to support a person 10 times or more its own weight. And that person is a highly dynamic load. He or she may sit, stand, twist, or shift on the chair, putting its joints and parts through strenuous cycles. Compare that with cabinets, chests, and dressers. This furniture is overbuilt relative to the weight it holds. A chest or dresser can easily weigh 50 to 100 pounds yet hold less than 30 pounds of clothing. Aside from sliding drawers, most of the time the load is stationary. You can see why chair joints fail, sometimes catastrophically.

One relatively easy solution for chairs that have only one loose joint is to bore a pocket hole in a discreet location, spread a thin film of professional-quality wood glue on the loose parts, and then drive a pocket screw to lock the joint together. If you try this with problematic chairs in your house, you'll be pleased with how well the repair stands up.

This technique won't work if there's adhesive from a previous repair on the joint; it creates an undesirable surface on which to spread new glue. And this works only for chairs with parts that are thick enough or wide enough to withstand the amount of wood that is removed when a pocket hole is bored. Finally, don't use this method on an antique; you could diminish its value.

With a chair that has a number of severely loose joints, label all the parts with masking tape, then disassemble them using a clamp with a reversible jaw, known as a spreader. After you have the parts separated, carefully scrape away the dried adhesive, then repair, rebuild, and reinforce the joints. Finally, reassemble the chair using professional-quality wood glue. If you're not an experienced woodworker, take a course at a community college or craft center before undertaking this project.

GADGETS

CHAPTER 05

YOU TAKE
TERRIBLE PHOTOS

Get to know your camera. Spending time with the user's manual won't kill you. Some cameras even display tips onscreen while you're shooting, as pop-ups or in help menus. Use the advice; you'll be glad you did.

Keep it clean. Smudges, specks of dirt, and other schmutz ruin a shot. Stash your camera in a case; buff the lens with a microfiber cloth.

BLURRY PHOTOS

If a lot of your photos are blurry, it's probably because you've been using your digital zoom. Most digital cameras have both optical zoom, in which the lens moves (just like a zoom on a film camera), and digital zoom, which manipulates the image electronically. The digital zoom can compromise the quality of the image. If you want more magnification than the optical zoom can handle, it's better to achieve it on a computer after the fact.

Balanced, centered, gaze-into-the-lens portraits are boring. So have the subject look off-frame, and use the rule of thirds: Imagine a tic-tac-toe grid within your camera frame and set your subject at one of the intersections. In a head-and-shoulders shot, align the subject's eyes with the top horizontal line of the (imaginary) grid. Also, get up close and personal. Capture one part of the body—eye, mouth, bare shoulder—because details can be telling. You don't need a zoom for this. In fact, we recommend that you use a prime lens, which has a fixed focal length.

With this type of lens, you zoom with your feet (step back or forward) to compose your shot within the frame. A prime lens also often has a low F-stop rating, which lets you achieve a shallow depth of field. Dial down the F-stop and pull your subject into focus. The background will blur, creating visual separation. Also regarding backgrounds: Avoid clutter. A neutral backdrop keeps the emphasis on the subject. And place your subject in an unusual setting. Shots that take people out of their comfort zone yield unexpected reactions. But don't go nuts: Asking your nephew to pose next to the bear is not okay.

On overcast days or in the shade, use your flash as a fill light to illuminate faces. Also, get a hot-shoe bounce flash if your camera supports it. A bounce flash lets you manipulate light by reflecting it off a ceiling or another bright surface. With a basic point-and-shoot camera, use a sheet of white paper to direct or diffuse light from a lamp or other source. Speaking of light, avoid having your subject look into bright sunlight, unless you like squinty eyes and ugly shadows. If you must shoot in a sunny setting, let the light fall at an angle across the person's face. But if you can wait, shoot just after sunrise or before sunset, when the light is softer and the colors warmer. When snapping pics of kids or pets, take a knee. Their cute mugs look even better when captured at their own height. Of course, you may also shoot high or low: Odd angles add drama.

Take your camera everywhere—the best photos aren't planned. And always bring extra batteries and memory cards. Having a camera with you that can't do the job is worse than having no camera at all. Now that you're fully equipped, shoot multiple shots at a time. The second or third shot—or the fifth one—when your subject begins to relax, can be the best one.

How to Fix a Bad Photo through Retouching

Color temperature: If the color adjustment can't fix unnatural colors, such as a sickly green from fluorescent lights, and there's no time to tweak the red, green, and blue levels, there's a last resort: Declare yourself an artist and switch the image's mode to black and white.

Cropping: Even a small spot of deep black or bright color can throw off a program's ability to balance an image's light or color levels. Crop out unwanted elements before making image-wide adjustments.

Lighting: Too much flash? Reduce the brightness and increase the contrast. For poorly lit images, do the opposite, boosting the brightness and reducing the contrast. To avoid gray, hazy images, make sure the photo's black elements are still black and the whites still white.

Red eye: Red eye is no longer an issue for most cameras. If you're using older equipment, and your software doesn't have red-eye reduction, zoom in on an offending eye until you can see pixels. Click the desaturation tool and dab at the red portion of each eye. This drains the color, while retaining highlights so the irises don't look artificial.

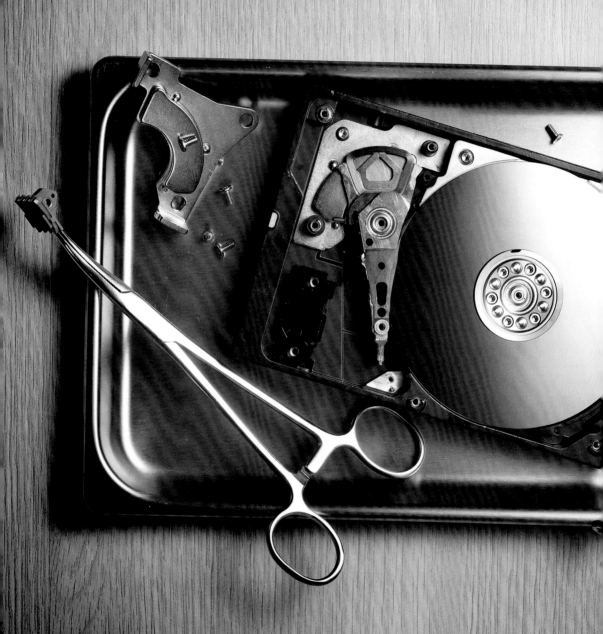

YOUR HARD DRIVE CRASHED

If you find yourself facing a data recovery job, you have probably forgotten the cardinal rule of computing: All hard drives eventually fail. And you didn't back up your data, did you? We've been there. Everybody has to learn this lesson once.

The first thing to do is determine if it really is a hard-drive failure you're confronting, and not one of the countless other equipment glitches that can cause a boot failure. If you have access to another computer, remove the failed hard drive from your sick PC, and hook it up as a secondary drive to the alternate computer. The easiest way to do this is through a USB universal drive adapter. It costs about $30 and is a good device to have around for all sorts of hard-drive diagnostics.

On a Mac, the process is simpler. Use a Thunderbolt cable to hook your nonworking Mac to a working Mac, then, "target boot" the nonworking machine by holding down the "T" key as you power it on. With either method, it's possible that your failed hard drive will show up on your healthy computer and reveal its files, in which case your hard drive is probably fine, but your operating system needs to be reinstalled. (Don't forget to offload your files before you do that.)

If your files don't show up on the secondary computer, then you are at one of those pivotal moments in life when you find out how much your hard work and treasured memories are really worth to you. Depending on how badly your drive is damaged, an attempt to salvage your data can cost anywhere from a few hundred dollars to several thousand. What's more, the process can take days—and there is no guarantee that the money and time you invest will produce any results whatsoever.

The good news: Very often, the data on failed drives is recoverable. In fact, it's surprising how resilient that information can be. Just ask any corporate embezzler who thought he had deleted all the evidence from his PC, only to have it show up later in court. The comparison is apt, since the very same computer forensic tools that uncover digital misdeeds are the ones that can find your treasured family photos.

There are two ways that drives crash: logical failure and mechanical failure. In a logical failure, the drive's components are physically undamaged, but because of either accidental formatting or a corrupt file system, the drive is not able to find and navigate its own data. However, unless it has been overwritten, that data still exists on your drive.

Your Laptop Touchpad Stopped Working

If your laptop's touchpad is giving you trouble, try dragging the corner of a note card around its edges. That should knock loose the crumbs and dust that are the likely culprits.

A mechanical failure means that your drive has broken parts that are preventing it from working—broken drives often make a telltale clicking sound as they futilely attempt to access their files. If you hear that, your data may still be there, but you're not getting it back without calling in the experts. And those experts make good money. If you are just dealing with a logical failure, however, you can get your files back on your own for far less.

Your first step there is to download the free demo diagnostic tool from Prosoft Engineering to check what might be salvageable. Many companies offer demos that will scan your drive and give you a pretty good idea of what's recoverable before you lay down money to buy their software. PC owners have far

more options, including Prosoft's Data Rescue PC, as well as Ontrack EasyRecovery DataRecovery and RecoverMyFiles from GetData.

Most of these products work in a similar way. Install the software, select the defective drive as your source, and choose a destination folder to receive the data. (Make sure your recovery drive has enough space for the contents of your failed drive.) Then be prepared to wait, and wait. A full scan and recovery takes days. Or longer.

Recovering a hard drive is a bit like getting back a stolen car—you'll be happy to have your files back, but the results could be messy. No data recovery program will return your files to you in exactly the condition you originally kept them. These programs are designed to essentially do a data dump from your problem drive to a new drive. Files will be organized by type (JPEG images will be in one folder, Word documents in some other folder, MPEG movies in another) and your songs and photos will be mixed with random sound and image files from your computer's system folder.

Additionally, the names of all your files will have been changed to various alphanumeric sequences, such as IMG1039.jpg or MOV2010.mov. So be prepared to settle in for a long weekend of sifting through and renaming your files. Maybe now's a good time to buy that backup drive.

YOUR HARD DRIVE GOT WET

If you want your data back, you're going to need a pro. Here's what she needs you to know so that she can do her job.

Don't plug in the drive. Don't test it or try to see if it's going to work. You'll only do more damage.

Put it in a plastic bag with a damp paper towel. This may seem counterintuitive, but keeping the drive moist may prevent the read/write heads from sticking to the media.

Check your insurance policy. Data recovery for a flooded drive can cost $2,000, but some policies have riders that cover it.

YOU GOT A COMPUTER VIRUS

UPDATE
First, check for operating system updates and patches. Most modern OSs offer automatic update support, but confirm that you have the latest version manually. Then update your security software. Check your firewall and router for updates as well, and, if necessary, reset the security settings to ensure your WiFi is locked down using WPA security.

ERADICATE
Run a full scan with your security software and delete any suspicious files it finds. Then make sure it is set up for scheduled scans. Some malware can open ports on your PC, allowing updated versions to pop in even after the real threat has been eradicated.

MONITOR
To make sure the demons are gone, run a program like ZoneAlarm (PC) or Little Snitch (Mac) to monitor incoming and outgoing data. At first, things will pop up that aren't threats; over time these programs learn your usage patterns. When you see a program or process displaying unusual activity, check the web to see if it's known malware.

REINSTALL
If you've got a bug that resists all attempts to remove it, you'll need to reinstall your system from scratch. Back up all your personal files to an external hard drive or the cloud, then reinstall your operating system. Move your old files back in and reinstall all your applications as well.

SCRATCHED SCREEN

There aren't a lot of good options, but there is one extreme choice: glass buffing. With a small drill attachment and a tub of cerium oxide compound (and for deep scratches, some sandpaper), it is possible to grind scratches out of a screen, the same way you would buff scratches out of auto glass. But be careful. Glass grinding requires the steady application of wet-mixed cerium oxide, which is quite messy, and sprayed water, a natural enemy of all things electronic. The best solution, short of screen replacement, is a screen-protector film. It won't just shield from future scratches—it will make some shallow ones invisible.

Wonky Autobrightness on Your Phone

You can recalibrate the phone's light sensors to make the screen brighten and dim properly. Apple's iOS allows you to adjust brightness levels on an iPhone even when autobrightness is turned on, so you can use built-in controls to get the sensors working again. To recalibrate the setting, turn autobrightness off in Display & Brightness settings. Then go into an unlit room and drag the adjustment slider to make the screen as dim as possible. Turn autobrightness on, and once you head back into the bright world, your phone should adjust itself. If it doesn't, follow the exact opposite procedure with a bright light, bringing up the brightness to its maximum level with autobrightness turned off and then turning it back on. Because Android devices make you choose between autobrightness and manual controls, you'll need an app to override the system's screen controls. Lux autobrightness provides the equivalent of iOS screen system settings, along with controls for specific apps and times of day.

YOUR ENTIRE PHONE IS ACTING UP

A reboot will fix most smartphone problems — if it's a hard reboot, which completely powers down the unit and restarts the hardware (a soft reboot only restarts the software). On most phones, you can trigger a hard reboot by holding down a specific combination of buttons. Do it occasionally to keep your phone running smoothly.

iPhone 7/7 Plus: Sleep/wake and volume down

iPhone 6 and earlier: Sleep/wake and home

Samsung Galaxy: Sleep/wake, home, and volume up

Motorola G4 and most Androids: Sleep/wake and volume down

VOLT/OHMMETER

This tool is far more versatile than its two-part name suggests. Aside from measuring voltage and resistance (ohms), it also measures current flow (amperage), and most modern versions emit a tone to signal a complete circuit (continuity).

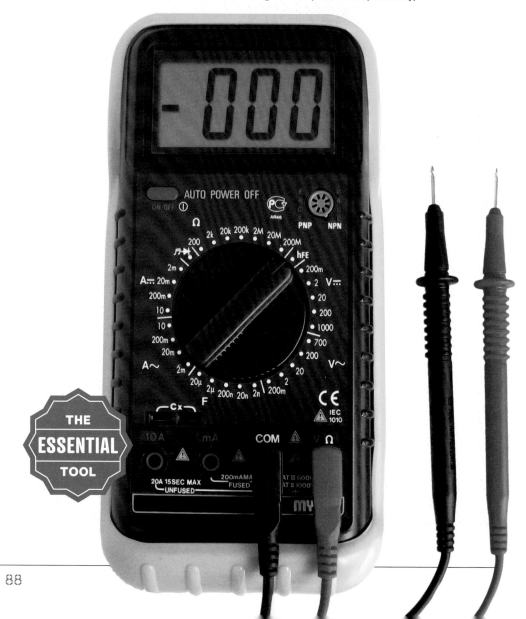

YOU CAN'T
HEAR CONVERSATIONS
ON YOUR PHONE

Dirt and dust can easily get trapped in the headphone jacks of many phones and laptop computers. On older iPhones that have headphones, dust can trip a sensor inside the jack, which tricks the phone into thinking headphones are plugged in and automatically mutes the phone's earpiece. So before you take a trip to the Apple store, try the MacGyver trick we picked up from luckow.com, the website of Al Luckow. Find a cotton swab. The Q-tip brand is good, simply because the cotton fluff tends to be less likely to shear off, but any should do. Cut off one end until only a tiny bit of cotton remains, just barely larger than the diameter of the swab axle. Dab a very small amount of rubbing alcohol on the shorn end. Slowly and gently ease the tip into the headphone jack and swish it around. Your goal is to remove any gunk that may be stuck in there.

FINNICKY HEADPHONE JACK

A headphone-jack socket gunked up with dust and pocket lint will make a fussy, staticky sound at a headphone cord's slightest movement. Clean it out with a blast from a can of air duster. If you're still having trouble, try licking the jack before reinserting it—saliva is conductive and can bridge a poor connection.

YOU CRASHED YOUR DRONE

You watched your fragile, complicated, expensive flying camera bounce between tree branches like a pachinko machine, then thud against the ground. Or maybe your drone refused to listen and shot out of sight into the sky. It happens to everyone. Everyone we know, at least. But what no one seemed to know was what to do about it. We kamikazeed a drone and found out.

OPTION 1: A REPAIR CENTER

Even if the damage looks minor, pay for an authorized shop. The crash may have knocked circuit boards loose, affecting much more than you see. Call the manufacturer or check its website to see if there's an authorized repair center anywhere near you. There are about a dozen scattered throughout the country. Only two do sanctioned DJI drone repairs. The rest work with Yuneec and other brands. The biggest benefit here will be turnaround time, which, compared to the huge queue you'll face when sending a drone back to the manufacturer (see Option 2), will take around two weeks instead of six or more. You're also more likely to deal with an invested human being.

OPTION 2: THE MANUFACTURER

Returning drones to the manufacturer can be a horrible experience—multimonth waits, indifferent customer service, warranty disputes—but if you don't have an authorized repair shop nearby, there's no better option. The huge facilities have factory parts and calibration software that ensure a proper repair. If you are among the 5 percent of pilots who crash due to build defects, not pilot error, and you're within the warranty, repairs are free. But don't expect to convince anyone that the crash wasn't your fault if it was. Drones have black boxes that record exactly what happened before a collision.

Some manufacturers have made the return process easier, providing an alternative to DJI's notoriously difficult customer service. EHang will repair a new Ghostdrone 2.0 VR up to three times within a year of purchase, and they claim that they'll do it with only a 10- to 14-day turnaround. Autel Robotics has live customer service on call seven days a week and two-week returns. Another option is to buy something like GoPro's two-year Care coverage ($149), which allows you to get your $800 Karma not just repaired but replaced for $199 with about a two-week wait. Even DJI came out with DJI Care ($219 for the Phantom 4), which will pay for repairs up to the value of the drone. Whatever drone you get, if the company offers insurance coverage, buy it.

OPTION 3: DO-IT-YOURSELF

If you clipped a propeller on a tree branch or cracked the camera component on a simple model, go ahead and replace it. Beyond that, don't try it. "You can replace a motor if you're good at soldering," says Werner von Stein, an engineer and head of the SF Drone School in San Francisco. "But if you had a pretty hard landing, it could be something else. When parts cost $600 or $700, it's better to replace the whole aircraft." If you want to try to repair it anyway, companies like Yuneec and Parrot sell parts directly. DJI doesn't sell as many parts, but you can buy scrap drones on eBay and use those components. And if you mess things up, well, you can get a little money selling your drone for scrap on eBay.

BASEMENT & MECHANICALS

CHAPTER 06

WATER PRESSURE
IS TOO HIGH

If you're getting a banging noise from the pipes every time you flush the toilet, try adjusting the pressure regulator before resorting to more expensive remedies, such as installing cushioning devices called water hammer arresters. In addition to causing the banging (a condition called water hammer), high water pressure can erode washers and result in leaks. It also creates premature wear on appliances, including your dishwasher and clothes washer.

The typical inlet water pressure to a home is about 40 to 45 psi. Normally, it should not exceed 60 psi. The pressure regulator is usually preset to 50 psi. However, it can be adjusted anywhere from 25 to 75 psi with a simple turn of a screw, as shown (left). To check the pressure, connect a pressure gauge to the nearest exterior faucet. These gauges are sold at home centers in the same area as in-ground sprinkler components.

Low Water Pressure

First, have the incoming water checked by the city water department to confirm that the pressure is okay. Once you know it's a problem in your house, the first thing to check for would be partially clogged faucet aerators at the bathroom and kitchen sink. Unscrew the aerators from the faucets, inspect them, and clean them, if necessary. If this doesn't help, then the low water flow is probably the result of a constriction in the distribution piping. Over the years, mineral and corrosive deposits form on the inside of iron pipes. This reduces the effective opening, which, in turn, reduces the flow at the faucets. If the rate of flow is unacceptable, the only solution is to replace the distribution piping and, in many cases, the inlet pipe.

THE ESSENTIAL TOOL

MACHINIST VISE

Whether stationary or swiveling, a vise is like an extra set of (really strong) hands for securing your work. Cast-iron models function well for most applications, but buy a forged-steel vise for anything heavy-duty. If you cut a lot of pipe, choose a vise with V-shaped jaws to grip round material. For moderate metal pounding, choose one with an anvil behind the jaws. While it's no substitute for a blacksmith anvil, it is handy for small projects.

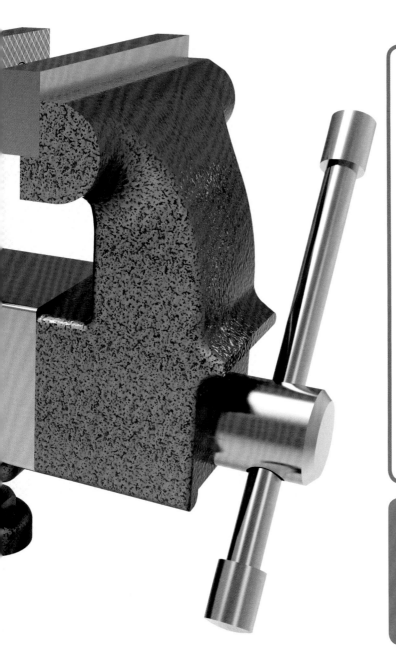

Broken Chain

When your chain suffers a broken link, a temporary fix avoids an immediate trip to the hardware store: Remove the broken link so that two disconnected-but-intact links remain. Select a nut and bolt whose shank fits throughout the chain links but whose head does not. Use it to join the two good links, reuniting the broken chain.

STUCK NUT

The standard tactic since the dawn of the acetylene torch has been to heat the nut until it glows red. When heat alone won't cut it, touch a candle to the glowing nut. The wax will melt and flow into the threads, acting as a lubricant.

ASK ROY

POPULAR MECHANICS' SENIOR HOME EDITOR SOLVES YOUR MOST PRESSING PROBLEMS.

We've got threaded steel pipe in the basement that leaks. My husband has taken it apart, wrapped it with tape, and put it back together. Twice. It still leaks. Can you help?

A When a threaded joint leaks, the natural response is to tighten it. Sometimes that stops the drip, but if you overtighten the joint, you could ruin the threaded parts and make the problem worse. Most likely only one of the pipe's fittings has stripped threads. To fix it, replace the pipe and bad fitting. There's no need to replace the fitting at the other end.

First, apply a generous amount of professional-grade pipe sealant, such as RectorSeal No. 5 to the male threads of the new pieces. Once the new pieces are as snug as you can get them with your bare hands, you need only a full turn to a turn and a half with tools. Hold the fitting or the pipe with one wrench, and with another turn the part you are tightening. Plumbers call this back holding. With RectorSeal you can send water through immediately.

Q: After a heavy rain, water leaks into my basement around the plastic conduit in the foundation wall. The conduit, which houses the inlet water pipe from the street, was surrounded with a foam-type material that I removed because it was wet. I tried to caulk the area to stop the leak, but the caulk didn't stick. How do I stop future leaks?

A: Use a hydraulic cement, such as UGL's Drylok Fast Plug. It comes as a powder that, when mixed with water, forms a mortarlike material. Unlike normal mortar that cures slowly, hydraulic cement sets within about 5 minutes. That's fast enough to seal a crack as water is seeping through it. Its primary use is for patching cracks and holes in foundations.

Hydraulic cement works best when applied to a relatively clean surface. Use a stainless steel wire brush to remove dust and loose material from the area, and peel off old caulk left from previous repairs.

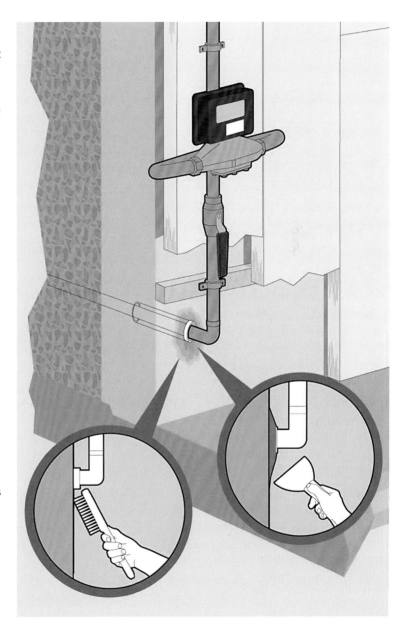

Q About 15 to 20 minutes after a large amount of hot water has been used, the pressure relief valve on the water heater discharges water. A plumber suggested installing an expansion tank in line with the water heater. I have never heard of this. Is the plumber's solution correct?

A As water is heated, it expands. In this case, the water's expansion is probably being limited by a backflow-preventer valve or a nonbypass pressure regulator on the water inlet pipe. This results in a pressure increase that can be reduced one of two ways—by someone drawing hot water from a tap, or by the relief valve opening on the water heater. In your case, the relief valve discharges after the hot-water demand has passed because the water heater's thermostat is still causing the electrical heating elements to be activated or the burner to fire. The heater is producing hot water but the hot-water faucets are closed, creating a pressure buildup that is relieved by the valve. The relief valve discharges after a large amount of water

is drawn because a small hot-water demand will not cause the heater's burner to fire or its element to be activated. Thermostats in residential water heaters let the water temperature drop 15–25°F before activating a burner or heating element.

Backflow preventers and nonbypass pressure regulators are valves that prevent contamination of a municipal water supply system. They stop water in the house's plumbing from flowing back into the municipal system. I agree with your plumber. Installing a precharged, bladder-type expansion tank on the cold-water inlet between the pressure regulator and the water heater should correct the problem. The expanding hot water pressurizes the air in the tank, as opposed to increasing the system's water pressure.

Your Hot Water Stinks

A domestic water heater basically consists of a lined steel tank. The lining is usually vitreous enamel (glass) but can be concrete (stone) or copper. Because the lining may have imperfections and pinholes, most heaters are equipped with a sacrificial magnesium anode rod that's suspended inside the tank to minimize tank corrosion. The electrochemical action that causes corrosion takes place between the water and the anode, rather than between the water and the tank. Therefore, the life of the tank is increased. Some tanks are constructed so that the magnesium anode can be replaced if necessary. The odor is probably the result of a reaction between the water and the magnesium anode. Water sometimes contains high sulfate and/or mineral content. These chemicals can react with the anode and produce a hydrogen sulfide or rotten-egg odor in the heated water. It's also possible that the odor is the result of the action on the anode of certain nonharmful bacteria in the water. In either case, chlorination of the water supply should eliminate or at least minimize the problem.

KNOCKING BASEBOARD HEAT

All piping materials expand and contract with temperature changes. A 50-foot length of copper pipe, any diameter, will expand in length more than $\frac{1}{2}$ inch when the water inside is raised from 70–170°F (typical for a baseboard radiator). This expansion can strain joints and cause leaks. It can also make elements bind against radiator covers and jam risers against floor holes, causing noise. Even when provisions are made during installation to absorb this expansion, some noise may still come from the baseboard units.

The noise is probably caused by the heat-distribution pipes or connecting fins rubbing on their support brackets as the pipes expand when the heat is coming up and as they contract when the heat is going down. This noise can usually be eliminated or reduced by inserting foam-rubber pads between the baseboard support brackets and the connector fins or distribution pipe, whichever is being supported. When inserting the pads, gently lift the heating pipes or fins. If you apply too much pressure, you will strain pipe joints and possibly crack them.

Sewage Smell in the Basement

This problem is common in homes where plumbing fixtures go unused for extended periods of time. More often than not, the fixtures are toilets or utility sinks in the basement, although it can happen with a fixture at any level. Lack of regular use results in the water evaporating from the fixture's trap. The water that's normally present in the trap provides a barrier against sewer gas entering the room. To correct this, pour some water down the drain to fill the trap. If you do this once a week, you should prevent the problem. In situations where there is a house trap on the main drain/waste pipe leading to the septic or municipal sewer, the condition is greatly reduced. Under normal conditions, there will be water in the house trap.

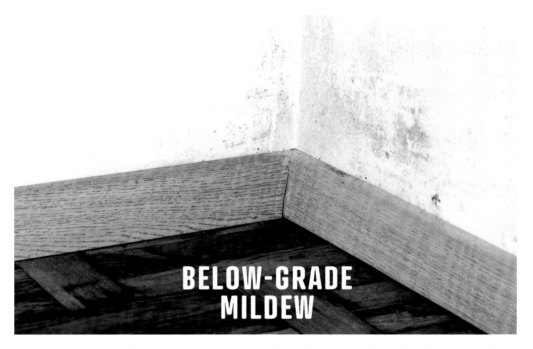

BELOW-GRADE MILDEW

When homes are built below grade, rooms on the lower floor can collect mildew, especially around the baseboards and occasionally on walls. Washing with a bleach solution will slow down the growth, but it won't always stop it. What you really need to do is control the dampness. When the dampness is the result of condensation of the warm, moist summer air, it can be controlled by a dehumidifier and ventilation. However, if the problem is caused mainly by moisture buildup on the foundation walls and floor slab because of the hydraulic pressure of wet soil adjacent to the house, additional measures must be taken.

If the house is built into the side of a hill, the most common cause is that the ground on the uphill side is not graded properly. The ground,

for at least several feet, should slope away from the house so surface water will not accumulate against the foundation. Also, gutters and drain pipes should channel roof rain runoff away from the house, and toward the downhill slope of the land, rather than letting it saturate the soil adjacent to the foundation.

If you can't always run a dehumidifier and fan, you might try getting rid of the dampness using chemicals that absorb moisture, such as silica gel and activated alumina. These chemicals can be placed in open containers or cloth bags in the problem areas. The chemicals have the capacity to absorb half their weight in water. After they have become saturated they can be heated to draw off the water, and then reused.

This ball-peen-hammer head looked dead before we removed the rust, polished the bare steel, applied a glassy enamel, and added a life-affirming new handle.

HOW TO RESTORE OLD TOOLS

Everybody has old, worn tools that could live useful lives again. To rescue one requires patience, sturdy abrasives—and vision. A neglected tool has an odd, magnetic power. It pulls you in. Pick it up and the next thing you know, you're scraping away rust with your thumbnail, trying to make out the manufacturer's name. You vaguely recall how you came by it: a tag sale, or your father-in-law, or a neighbor who was moving away. "Restoring them is pretty easy," says contributing editor Richard Romanski, a fine woodworker and unrepentant tool collector. We gathered a bunch of forlorn implements and went to work in his studio, a cavernous former church in North Salem, New York. We found that all it takes is some basic chemistry and a little work to salvage tools that look like they've been sitting on the bottom of the ocean for a century or two.

TARGET: A RUSTY, WOBBLY TABLE SAW

Even a good machine can be rendered inoperative by a little rust and parts that go out of alignment or calibration.

A table saw that earns its keep in an unheated garage, shop, or barn will soon rust. Condensation forms on its steel and cast-iron parts because they are cooler than the surrounding air **(1)**. The rust makes it difficult to slide plywood across the table, which should be smooth and nonabrasive. It also makes it hard to raise and lower the blade or adjust its tilt. This early 1980s Craftsman saw cost $80 at a church auction. Its table was rusty, and its parts had been thrown out of alignment.

The first step was to move the saw to a warm, dry workshop. We took it off its rolling stand and hoisted it into a Ford F-150, then drove it down the street to Romanski's studio **(2)**.

Next came disassembly. We unbolted the cast-iron wings from each side of the saw and removed the motor **(3)**. We were pleased to find that the motor was a commercial-duty type with twin capacitors—one to start the motor turning and another to provide extra kick to the run winding. The motor's shaft and pulley were all in good shape. We used compressed air to blow accumulated sawdust and cobwebs out of the saw's cavity **(4)**.

Next came removal of surface rust from the saw's table and wings. We wet down the surface with kerosene as a cutting lubricant and left it alone to penetrate while we ate lunch. To buff the rust away, we chucked up a variable-speed electric drill with a 2½-inch abrasive nylon cup brush embedded with 240-grit aluminum oxide. At a low 500 rpm, with a back-and-forth movement, the brush removed the rust without marring the surface.

We mounted the wings back on the saw and found that we could align them with the saw table by flexing them slightly and carefully tapping them into position with a dead-blow hammer. After placing a new 10-inch carbide

The Machine: Craftsman table saw, circa 1980s, purchased at a church auction for $80
The Equipment: Adjustable wrenches for disassembly, air compressor to remove debris, kerosene and a half-inch drill with wire cup brush for the rust, dead-blow hammer, rulers, machinist's square

blade on the arbor (the shaft the blade goes on), Romanski used a machinist's square to ensure the blade was perpendicular to the table. With the blade at 90 degrees, the pointer on the saw's tilt scale should read 0 degrees—if not, the pointer is moved to the zero mark. Next we adjusted the fence and its locking mechanism to make it snug, a fussy trial-and-error process. With the saw blade raised to its full height, we used a pair of steel rulers to check that the fence was parallel to the blade at the front and back **(5)**.

The tuneup was completed when Romanski reinstalled the motor and used a long steel ruler to align its pulley with the pulley on the saw's arbor shaft. We buffed on a coat of paste wax to provide rust protection and bolted the saw to its stand. Once it was in place, we made a few test cuts on some scrap pine to check for alignment. It was perfect **(6)**.

TARGET: CORRODED HAND TOOLS

Tools grow dull, and when they grow dull they are set aside, and when they are set aside they rust. And rust begets more rust, until they look like these. Time to dig in.

Rusty tools turn up in the garden shed of the house you just bought. A friend gives you a boxful of them. Often their handles are rotted away and their steel is so rusty that you could get tetanus just by looking at them.

To restore a pile of ball-peen-hammer heads and a couple of hatchets, we first removed what was left of their handles. We sawed off the handle stubs using a handsaw, then clamped each head in a machinist's vise and used a punch to knock out the remainder of the handle.

Corrosion removal began in earnest when we submerged the heads in a bucket containing 1 gallon of white vinegar, an inexpensive supermarket item. We covered the bucket with a piece of plywood and let the parts soak. After about four hours, we took a few out and tried scrubbing off the rust with No. 1 steel wool **(7)**, and wouldn't you know it, a little came off. There was hope. We dunked the tools back in the vinegar overnight, then hit them again with steel wool. (Steel wool is available in eight grades of coarseness, ranging from superfine, No. 0000, to extra-coarse, No. 4. We had good results with No. 1 wool, but you may need to go more or less coarse, depending on the amount of corrosion.)

The rust came off. We rinsed the tools thoroughly in clear water to remove any last trace of vinegar and wiped them dry.

Severely pitted surfaces were then smoothed out using a 100-grit abrasive on a disc sander, and heinous damage—metal that had been peened over by a hammer blow, for example—was rectified by clamping the head in a machinist's vise and hand-filing the surface smooth. Finally, the tools were wiped clean with mineral spirits, primed with a rust-preventive metal primer (we used spray-on Rust-Oleum), and painted with a gloss alkyd enamel. Cutting edges on the hatchets were hand-honed on a series of water stones used for woodworking tools. We completed the repair on each tool by fitting a hickory handle through the cavity in the head.

DULL PRECISION TOOLS

Hand planes, mechanist's square, and adjustable combination squares are precision tools that require careful—okay, fussy—restoration and adjustment.

Begin restoring any precision tool with a careful disassembly, separating corroded parts from the clean ones **(8)**. In the case of the smooth plane pictured here, the body was not as badly corroded as it looked. We removed most of the rust with a hand wire brush. Then we lapped the sole of the plane on a succession of abrasive papers, beginning with 60-grit and proceeding through 1,000-grit. We taped the paper to a workbench that has a dead-flat laminate surface and slid the plane body over the paper, swapping it end for end every six passes. We used a few drops of odorless mineral spirits as our cutting lubricant. The body came out flat and smooth, with only minor pitting.

Next we sharpened the plane iron on a horizontal wet sharp-

THE TOOL: Stanley hand plane, circa 1960s
THE EQUIPMENT: Wire brush, sandpaper, mineral spirits, wet polishing wheel, muslin buffing wheel with polishing compound, water stones

12

ening wheel and even honed its back surface so that it was flat several inches behind the cutting edge **(9)**. This ensures that the chip breaker will tightly mount to it and not allow wood shavings to be trapped and torn off. After sharpening, we took the lever cap and the plane iron's chip breaker and buffed them out on a muslin buffing wheel with jewelers red rouge polishing compound **(10)**.

Romanski has more than forty years of woodworking experience, so he did the final inspection of the plane iron **(11)**. He followed the machine honing with a careful trip over his water stones, leaving the plane iron with a mirror finish. He assembled and adjusted the plane and took it for a test drive on a piece of clear white pine. The result was a tool that cuts perfectly, taking long, silky-smooth shavings with every pass **(12)**.

Pipe

	Galvanized Steel	Copper	Polyvinyl Chloride (PVC)	Cross-Linked Polyethylene (PEX)	Poly-Propylene (PP)
ADVANTAGES	Inexpensive, durable	Lightweight, corrosion-resistant	Inexpensive, lightweight, easy to use	Flexible, easy to join, lower propensity to leak	Durable, minimal risk of chemical exposure
DISADVANTAGES	Develops lime deposits in alkaline water	Expensive, may require soldering tools, may get stolen	Limited to uses that stay below 140°F, like drainage and wastewater	Damaged by UV light	Expensive, requires special tools
JOINING	Pipe is threaded, and joints are sealed with pipe-joint compound or tape.	Traditionally soldered, but modern compression fittings create solderless joints, though they sometimes require special tools.	Cut pipe to length with a saw; join to fittings with adhesive. Also accepts compression fittings, like copper.	After a fitting has been inserted into the pipe, a special crimping tool clamps a ring around it, forming a seal.	A heating tool is used to semi-liquefy the ends of the pipe to be joined. They are then hand-pressed together.

Fittings

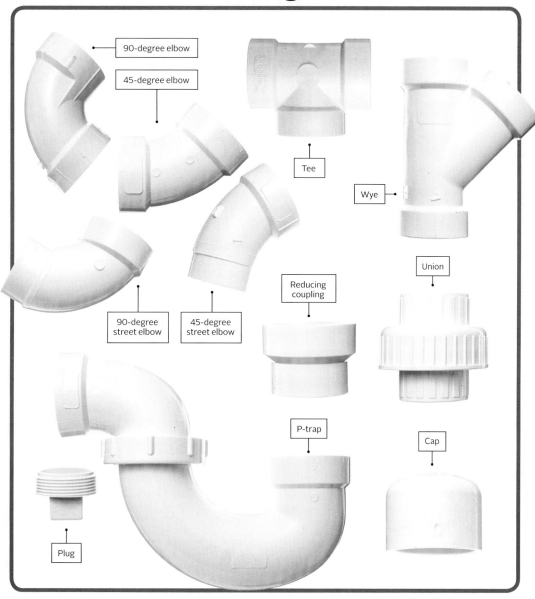

90-degree elbow

45-degree elbow

Tee

Wye

90-degree street elbow

45-degree street elbow

Reducing coupling

Union

P-trap

Cap

Plug

CRAWLSPACE IS WET

With a concrete slab, if there are separate areas of ponded water, you can use a wet/dry shop vacuum to take up the water. It's not easy work in a crawlspace, but it can be done. If the water is covering the entire floor or a large area, you can get the water out with a pool cover pump. This pump is particularly well-suited for this because it's designed to quickly pump out a large but shallow area and discharge through a garden hose. It comes with a 24-foot cord that should be plugged into a GFCI outlet or a GFCI-protected extension cord. The pump will remove 1,800 gallons of water per hour and bring the water level down to less than ½ inch, at which point you can finish the job with a shop vac.

If the crawlspace has a dirt floor, let the water percolate out. When the space is dry, cover the ground with a 4-mil polyethylene sheet to prevent the moisture vapor in the soil from rising into the house. Overlap the sheets by a minimum of 6 inches; they should be turned up onto the foundation wall and fastened to it with plastic tape.

Whatever floor you have, the real key is prevention. Gutter runoff should flow out of the downspouts and discharge at least 10 feet from the foundation. The ground surrounding the foundation should slope away from it on all sides. Finally, there must be a gravel-and-pipe foundation drain system, and it should not be blocked or broken.

BASEMENT DRAIN SMELLS

The water in the drain trap probably dried up and is no longer blocking sewer gas. Pour nontoxic plumbing antifreeze down the drain to fill the trap. You can use water in a pinch, but it evaporates faster than antifreeze, so you'll need to repeat the process more often.

BROKEN CHRISTMAS LIGHTS

First step: Diagnosis. You need to figure out if it's actually a bad bulb causing the malfunction or something else. Keep in mind that smaller sets are wired in series. The current must pass through each bulb in order to complete the circuit. Larger strings often feature two or more series circuits wired in parallel, which explains why sometimes just a section of the strand won't light up. Oftentimes, replacing a bad bulb will fix a section or the entire set.

But locating the faulty bulb can be tricky. You'll need either a set of basic electrician's tools or the LightKeeper Pro, a dedicated tool that combines a voltage detector, a bulb remover, bulb and fuse testers, and a shunt repairer. If you're lucky, simply plugging in the mini lights will reveal a bad bulb. "Bad" may just mean it needs to be seated more firmly in its socket. In any case, you can remove and test a bulb using the LightKeeper Pro or a multi-meter. If you install a new one, make sure it has the proper voltage rating or you'll risk damaging the whole set.

Sometimes it's not as easy as that. All or part of the string may be dark because of a broken filament or a sketchy shunt—the aluminum wire wrapped around the copper posts at the base of the bulb. If a bulb's filament breaks, the shunt is supposed to redirect current through the base of the bulb, maintaining the electrical circuit. You can fix a faulty shunt with the LightKeeper Pro. Simply plug in the strand, remove a bulb that's in or near the darkened section, and insert the tool into the bulb's socket. Pulling the trigger activates a piezo circuit, which sends a high-energy pulse through the set. After about 20 pulses, any faulty shunt should be activated.

If you're still having trouble locating where the circuit is broken, try a voltage detector. Still nothing? Check the fuse that's behind a panel on the male plug. If it's fried, replace it with a new one of the correct rating, which should be indicated on the plug.

GARAGE & DRIVEWAY

CHAPTER 07

FLAT BIKE TIRE

Once you remove the wheel, force the deflated tire off the rim, starting opposite the valve, then separate tire and tube. If the leak is a large tear, throw the tube out. To locate a pinhole leak, inflate the tube and feel for escaping air. If necessary, dunk the tube in water and look for bubbles. Apply a patch from the kit you should always bring along when biking. The repair should last the life of the tire. Before remounting the tire, wipe the inside of it clean with a dry cloth to remove any sharp objects that might puncture the tube. Then work the lip of the tire onto half of the rim. Tuck the tube inside the tire, and insert the valve into its rim hole. Pump some air into the tube to reduce its chances of getting pinched between rim and tire. Then work the tire onto the rest of the rim, starting at the valve. Split the wheel into quarters. Work one-quarter down either side from the valve. Then repeat the process on the other half of the tire. This final step may require two bike levers.

YOU DON'T HAVE A REPLACEMENT INNER TUBE

You can create a makeshift inner tube out of leaves and grass. Leave one side of the tire bead hooked on the rim, and cram the opening with as much soft stuff as you can find. Install the other bead. At least it will get you home.

POOLING IN DRIVEWAY

A knowledgeable contractor can cut out sunken concrete that's causing water to pool and install a new slab without damaging surrounding concrete. The job can get tricky, however, if there's not enough room for a masonry saw at one or more edges. That can happen in corners where a slab meets a foundation wall or another slab. The color of the replacement piece won't match that of the surrounding concrete, although this can be mitigated by using concrete stain on the entire driveway.

An alternative to cutting and removal is slab jacking (also known as mud jacking). A contractor uses a rock drill or a core drill (a hole saw for masonry) to make some holes in the sunken slab **(1)**. Then he pumps a material called grout through the hole **(2)**. This is like concrete, but it lacks coarse aggregate, such as stone or gravel. As this material is forced under the slab, it lifts the slab up. After the slab is lifted, the holes are filled with more grout or a concrete patching compound **(3)**, or the concrete cores are glued back into place with a specialized adhesive. There's an obvious environmental benefit to this procedure. It takes less energy and materials to jack up a slab than to replace it and pulverize the old concrete for use as roadbuilding material. The process generates very little debris to dispose of, an obvious benefit in areas where there is little or no concrete recycling.

SLICK GARAGE FLOOR

"From an engineering point of view, there's required friction [the friction a person needs to walk safely] and the available friction [the friction the floor surface presents to the person]," says April Chambers, director at the University of Pittsburgh's Human Movement and Balance Laboratory. "Your first goal to prevent a slipping accident is to ensure that available friction is greater than required friction." Translation: Add friction, add safety.

How aggressively you treat the surface depends on the severity of the slip hazard. In the case of your garage floor, treat it very aggressively, because a smooth concrete surface that has slush and water on it is almost as slippery as a surface can get. One solution is to apply rows of nonslip tape that has very coarse, abrasive particles bonded to its face. One of the best is 3M's Safety-Walk; it's available in vari-

ous levels of coarseness to suit the specifics of the application. We use the 700 series because it has the roughest surface and it resists moisture. You can also use it on the footing surfaces of tractors and trailers and on boat decks and docks. Porous surfaces need to be sealed with 3M Safety-Walk primer before the tape is applied.

Chambers cautions, however, that you never want to increase friction in a manner that creates a false sense of security. That is, taping one section of a slippery floor but not another can actually increase the chance of a fall as someone steps from a secure, high-friction surface to one that's slippery. A good way to uniformly increase the friction of a large area is to add abrasive particles to floor paint. Skid-Tex is a fine-grained silica sand that you can add to floor paint at the ratio of 1 pound per gallon. You simply stir it in and then paint as normal.

Oil-Stained Floors

Mix a double handful of kitty litter and a quarter cup of laundry detergent in some sort of container, adding enough water to make the resulting slurry the consistency of gravy. Cover the stain with this slurry. Allow it to dry thoroughly, then sweep it up.

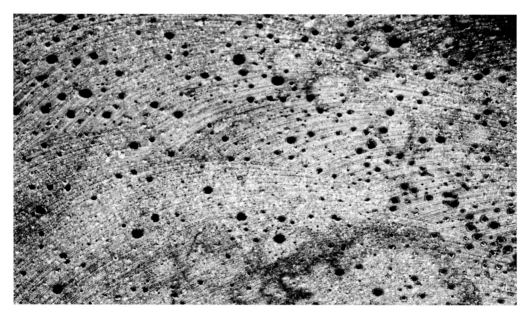

PROBLEMS WITH CONCRETE

SLIPPERY CONCRETE

Two do-it-yourself methods for reducing the slipperiness of something like a concrete basketball court would be to paint it with a nonslip outdoor paint or to roughen it. The paint, however, may lift or be worn away in areas near the hoop, so roughening the slab may be more attractive. There are two ways to do this: sandblasting and acid-washing. We hesitate to recommend the former, because it is extremely messy—and expensive, since it requires the services of a sandblasting contractor. Acid-washing the surface removes some of the cement paste and exposes more of the sand in the concrete. This results in a grittier texture that is similar to a medium grade of sandpaper.

Acid-washing is done with muriatic acid and water. This acid is sold at hardware stores and home centers. Combine 1 part acid with $2\frac{1}{2}$ to 3 parts clean, cool water. Wear old clothing, rubber gloves, and a face shield when working with muriatic acid. Never pour the water into the acid. Instead, add the acid to the water. Use 1 gallon of the mixture for every 50 to 60 square feet of court area.

Prior to acid-washing, prepare the basketball court surface by washing it with clean water. While the concrete is damp, spread the acid mixture over the area by carefully pouring it from the container. Use a stiff-bristle broom or driveway squeegee to move the mixture over the concrete. The acid solution will bubble and foam as it etches the concrete. Apply more mixture in places where little of this reaction is occurring. The goal is to etch the surface evenly.

After about 20 to 30 minutes, remove the acid/water mixture by thoroughly washing down the area with fresh water. If the surface texture is not as gritty as desired, repeat the process. The process may damage the lawn adjacent to the court. In this case, fertilizing and seeding will be necessary.

DISCOLORED CONCRETE

A fungus causes spotted black areas—typically a sign of mildew—and any rust-color stains are iron oxide, which may come from a lawn sprinkler, lawn fertilizer, or iron particles in the concrete. According to the Portland Cement Association (PCA), a solution for removing mildew from concrete is: 1 ounce of laundry detergent, 3 ounces of trisodium phosphate, 1 quart of laundry bleach, and 3 quarts of water. Apply this to the area with a soft brush and let it stand. Then hose down the area. The rust stains can be removed with a solution of 1 pound oxalic acid per gallon of water. Rinse the area off after 3 hours, using clean water and by scrubbing with a stiff-bristle broom. Oxalic acid, otherwise known as wood bleach, is sold at hardware stores, paint stores, and from some woodworking supply catalogs.

PAINT MIST ON CONCRETE

If the mist from a paint sprayer got on your concrete, but it's slight, then foot traffic and weather will slowly remove it. If the walk has a substantial amount of paint on it, then try applying a paste made with gelled commercial paint remover and talcum powder. Leave the paste in place for 30 minutes, and then gently scrub the area to loosen the paint particles and wash them off with water. It may be necessary to repeat the treatment.

SPALLED CONCRETE ON GARAGE FLOOR

These spalled sections are typically caused by deicing salts dripping from a car. There are a number of materials for patching. The area to be patched should be roughened by sandblasting or chipping to about 12 inches beyond the spall. The area should be clean and dry. Remove oil and grease, loose concrete, and dust. Make sure there is no moisture rising through the concrete. Since epoxy products vary, follow the manufacturer's directions.

Depending on the size of the spalled area, it may be more economical to use a concrete mix. However, this will require more surface preparation, since concrete cannot be "feathered" out like epoxy. The edges of the area to be patched must be undercut to hold the mix in place. The procedure outlined below for patching a floor is from the American Concrete Institute's booklet *Slabs on Grade*.

1. Using a circular saw with a masonry (silicon-carbide) blade, make a rectangle of outward-angled, $\frac{1}{2}$-inch-deep cuts around the spalled area.
2. Wearing goggles, chip concrete within the saw-cut area to about $1\frac{1}{2}$ inches deep, using a cold chisel. The chipped surface should be rough but clean.
3. Dampen the area with water, cover with wet burlap, and allow it to stand for several hours.
4. Mix concrete for the patch in the same proportions as the slab. If you don't know the mix of the original concrete, use a ratio of $5\frac{1}{2}$ gallons of water per 94-pound bag of cement. Let the mix stand several minutes before placing it in the patch.
5. Remove excess water from the patch area, but leave the surface damp.
6. Compact concrete into the patch, overfilling slightly.
7. After a few minutes, level it to match the surrounding surface, then finish to the required texture.
8. Keep the patch damp for three days.

ASK ROY

POPULAR MECHANICS' SENIOR HOME EDITOR SOLVES YOUR MOST PRESSING PROBLEMS.

(Q)

A gap has developed where the concrete walk leading to my front door meets the sidewalk. What can I use to fill the gap?

(A) The joint where the two walks meet is known as an isolation joint. It isolates the two concrete structures from one another and allows them to move independently without damaging each other. When the house's front walk was poured, the mason installed a length of isolation joint material between the front walk and the sidewalk. Over time, that material has eroded. The gap left by it can fill with water that freezes in the winter and dirt that supports summer weed growth. Over time, the weed growth and the freeze/thaw cycle can actually damage the concrete edges.

Here's how to do the repair: First pry any remaining isolation joint material out with an old screwdriver or chop it out of the joint with a narrow cold chisel struck by a ball-peen

hammer. Next, flush loose debris from the joint with a garden hose. When the concrete is dry, use a wire brush to remove moss and dirt on the inside edges of the concrete. Brush away any loose dust when you're done. Now press a piece of foam backer rod into the opening. This flexible material is sold in coils in various diameters and lengths. Choose one that fills the gap completely and presses against the concrete on both sides.

Apply a layer of polyurethane self-leveling sealant above the backer rod. To achieve maximum durability, the shape of the cured sealant should have specific proportions. For example, Quikrete polyurethane self-leveling sealant is used on joints no wider than $\frac{1}{2}$ inch with a depth of $\frac{1}{4}$ to $\frac{3}{8}$ inch. Visit quikrete.com for more information.

DRIED OUT
ASPHALT DRIVEWAY

Whether or not you should seal your driveway depends on its condition. If it exhibits extensive cracking, sealing it will not prolong its life because the sealer will not bridge the cracks; it will only change the appearance of the driveway. On the other hand, as long as the driveway surface is in reasonably good condition, it should be sealed every one to three years, depending on the severity of the climate. Small cracks should be cleaned out with a wire brush or compressed air and then filled with a crack-filling material. Then the driveway should be sealed.

It's best to seal driveways when they are less than a year old, although they can be sealed successfully years later. Bear in mind that a new asphalt driveway is flexible and elastic. It will expand and contract without cracking. As a driveway ages, however, the pavement loses its elasticity and becomes brittle and vulnerable to cracking.

When water enters cracks in asphalt, it works its way down to the base below, reducing the base's compressive strength. This can cause depressions to form and, eventually, potholes. If the water freezes, the ice can increase the size of the cracks. Also, a coat of sealer protects the driveway from damage caused by the sun's rays, and if the sealer is a coal-tar emulsion, it will protect the driveway from surface unraveling caused by oil drips or gasoline spills. In cold climates, sand is added to the sealer to provide slip resistance.

If a contractor is going to seal your driveway, do the following: Check to see if that person is licensed, and call the local consumer protection office to find out if there are any complaints against that contractor. Ask the contractor what proportion of the sealer is coal tar. It should be about 70 percent coal tar and 30 percent water. Typically, the 5-gallon drums of coal-tar driveway sealer that a homeowner buys at a home center or hardware store are 50–70 percent water and 30–40 percent coal tar. Lastly, ask if the sealing is done by hand or is sprayed on. A sprayed coat of sealer is more uniform in its thickness and its appearance. Sealer applied by brush, roller, or squeegee may exhibit some surface imperfections, such as brush marks or ridges.

THE
ESSENTIAL
TOOL

SOCKET WRENCH SET

Reach for a socket wrench when you need to tighten fasteners or loosen frozen ones. The ½-inch drive is the heavy hitter of the socket wrench kingdom, followed by a switch hitter, the ⅜-inch drive, which is big enough to do light-duty automotive work yet small enough for some appliances. Reserve the ¼-inch drive for appliance and electronics repair.

DAMAGED FUEL LINE IN A CAR

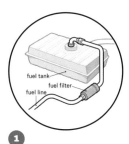   

1

Find the leak.
If a spot of gas appears on the driveway, you've got a fuel-line leak. To find it, jack up the vehicle and scan the steel fuel line that runs from your gas tank to the engine for holes. There will be multiple sections—for example, between the gas tank and the fuel filter, and between the filter and the pump. Note, however, that fuel line damage is usually caused by rust, so it is often found near the fittings that attach the line to the tank or the fuel filter. Use the location of the gas spot on the pavement to help you locate the damage.

2

Remove the line.
Detach the damaged section by unlatching the clasps that hold the line to the underside of the car. Using tape or chalk, mark the path of the line and where the clasps should go. Most late-model vehicles have brass fittings that connect sections of the fuel line, but some older vehicles use flexible hose instead. The former often require a tubing wrench and can be challenging to remove because of age and corrosion. When working on these, keep a can of penetrating oil such as PB B'laster handy.

3

Buy a new fuel filter and line.
Lots of shops bend their own fuel lines, but you can also buy prebent line. While you're at it, pick up a new fuel filter. The only information the store clerks need to help you find both of these items is your car's vehicle identification number, located on a label, which is typically attached to the inner part of your door.

4

Install everything.
If possible, ask a friend to hold the line while you attach it, then use the old clips or a set of new ones to secure it to the car's underside. Make sure to connect it to the same components it was connected to before. Also, bolt on the new fuel filter in the correct direction. You may have to note the direction before you remove the old one, or check for an arrow on the new filter. Now start your vehicle. Once fuel cycles through the system a few times, if there are any problems, they should be obvious.

Leaking Oil Pan

Whittle a plug from a twig and hammer it into the hole. Trim off the excess so the plug doesn't catch on the next rock. But now you don't have enough oil to refill the crankcase. Add a quart of water. Really. The oil-pump pickup is not on the exact bottom—the remaining oil will float on top of the water.

Loose Seat-Belt Tensioner

Check for contamination. The protective housing is not airtight, and if you do a lot of dusty driving, the cup or the bearing could easily become caked with dirt over the years. That could keep the bearing from rolling properly. Address this by popping the trim off the B-pillar and then unbolting the seat-belt recoil mechanism from the car (it's just one bolt). Pry the lock mechanism's protective translucent cover loose with a standard screwdriver, and then clean the cup and the bearing with a soap-and-water solution. Let it dry thoroughly, and reinstall the mechanism with a dab of Loctite on the threads of the retaining bolt. Test the belt to see if it works. If it's still stubborn, just get a new one from the dealership. There's no need to entrust your safety to a compromised device.

Tapes

A / ELECTRICIAN'S PUTTY

What it is: Synthetic rubber compounds, carbon black, granular filler on peel-off backing

What it's for: Starts as tape, molds into putty; forms around cable and pipe where they pass through siding, framing; blocks water and bugs and other vermin

B / GLUE STRIP

What it is: Wax paper with adhesive bead

What it's for: Peel-off paper backing leaves 1/16-inch-wide glue strip for light-duty fastening, such as attaching small pieces of wood trim

C / DUCT

What it is: Fiber-reinforced plastic (7.7 to 12.6 mils thick) with rubber or synthetic rubber adhesive

What it's for: The thin, inexpensive type is ideal for strapping, bundling, patching tarp, and for light-duty rope whipping, which prevents a rope's tendency to fray. The professional, heavy-duty variety is appropriate for duct sealing. Both types damage a substrate when peeled away.

D / ELECTRICAL

What it is: Vinyl or PVC (7 to 8.5 mils thick) with adhesive that ranges from mildly to extremely sticky

What it's for: Small indoor electrical repairs can be made with the thinner variety. For outdoor use, buy the heavier, stretchable stuff.

E / SELF-FUSING RUBBER

What it is: Silicone rubber (20 to 30 mils thick) with peel-off backing

What it's for: Repairs and wraps hoses, electrical cable, tool and sport equipment handles; flexible, stretchable

F / MASKING (GENERAL)

What it is: Crepe paper (4.5 to 5.5 mils thick) with rubber or acrylic adhesive

What it's for: Invented by 3M in 1925, it bundles materials and fastens paper. Note: Sunlight bakes tape onto surfaces, making removal difficult.

G / MASKING (PAINTING AND HEAVY-DUTY)

What it is: Crepe paper (5.7 to nearly 8 mils thick) with rubber adhesive duck masking tape

What it's for: Used indoors or out, heavy-duty varieties of this tape are suited for high temperatures and rough surfaces. Removal period ranges from 7 to 14 days.

QUICK FIX:

LEAK IN A RADIATOR HOSE

Wait for the engine to cool off. Open the hood and locate the source of the steam—i.e., the rupture (**1**). Clean and dry the area around the fissure; the tape won't stick as well on a damp, dirty surface. Wrap 2 to 3 inches of duct tape around the hose over the hole; press firmly (**2**). Overwrap the patch (the hose will be under intense pressure) from 2 to 3 inches above the original piece to about 2 or 3 inches below, then work your way back (**3**). Check your radiator level before cranking the engine. If it's seriously low and you don't have any coolant, you can use water. In an emergency, diet soda works, too. Just don't use fruit juice. The sugar and acids can corrode the radiator and hoses.

Overheating Engine

Turn the heater on full blast (opening the windows so you don't fry). The extra volume of the heater core and its hoses, as well as the airflow of the heater fan blowing across the core, may dissipate enough heat to get you home—or to the garage—without a meltdown.

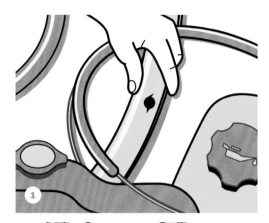

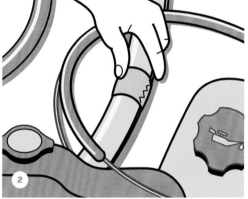

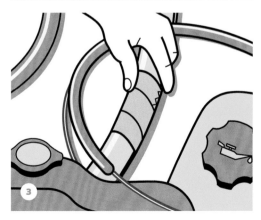

BROKEN REAR DEFROSTER

Resistance wires are silk-screened, essentially painted, onto the glass. They are very easy to scratch, and will not work properly if the scratch breaks the continuity along the wire. This means that it's possible for boxes, furniture, or any other hard object one might place in a car to scratch the wire. Even a credit card can damage it. Don't cram stuff into the back, and don't let the load shift backward in your minivan so that it touches the glass. If your window has a defroster grid, the only thing that should ever touch the glass is a soft cloth dampened with window cleaner. If you must clean the rear glass, scrub gently, and in the direction of the grid, not across it.

ELECTRICAL ISSUES

First, check the obvious: Is the fuse okay? Defroster grids draw a lot of current (10 to 20 amps), and if the fuse is undersize, it won't last. If the fuse doesn't look blown, check with your voltmeter—with the ignition on and the defroster on, you should see 12 volts at both fuse terminals.

If the voltage is fine, the problem is somewhere in the wiring or at the grid. Check the connections from the wiring harness to the grid. It's easy for the terminals at the grid to become damaged. Generally, the tab that's attached to the glass breaks off, leaving you with a dangling wire and no way to reattach it. You have two repair options here: soldering and gluing.

If you know how to solder and have a high-capacity soldering iron or gun, solder the tab back on. It may take a third hand to hold the tab against the grid while you solder it. There's usually a metal strip laid on the glass under the silk-screening. Clean the surfaces with alcohol and use 60-40 rosin-core solder. Work fast, because excess heat may crack the glass.

If you aren't confident about your soldering skills, or you aren't ready to take a chance on cracking an expensive piece of glass, there's another way. The dealership and most auto parts stores can sell you a special electrically conductive epoxy to bond the tab back on. If it's wintertime, you'll need to work in a heated garage, and have the vehicle inside long enough for it to warm up to at least 65°F. Again, clean the area with alcohol. Mask the glass with tape to keep from getting epoxy smeared on it. Mix up a sparing amount of epoxy and hardener. Put some epoxy on the tab, and use an ice pick to hold it in place for the 10 minutes or so it will take for the epoxy to harden. You can use a wooden stick or the end of your dampened finger to smear the epoxy within a minute or two of application to improve the cosmetics of the repair. Although the epoxy will set up rapidly, don't attempt to reattach the wiring until it's had 24 hours at 65°F or more to cure and achieve its full strength. The repair will never be as strong as the original wire, so you'll need to be particularly careful not to damage it in the future.

WIRING

If the grid is attached to the glass but you're getting no defrosting action, look for a bad switch, relay, or timer. For this you'll need a schematic diagram, or considerable experience in troubleshooting wiring problems. Start at the fuse and trace the wiring. If the switch is bad, you'll be able to jumper the switch and get 12 volts beyond there for diagnosis. But you may need to replace the timer—which may be integrated into a larger box of electrical controls buried under the dash. Consult the owner's manual. If that isn't available to you, you'll have to find the problem the old-fashioned way. Trace the current path from the fuse, to the switch, to the timer, and on back to the window. Remember, the timer will turn off the current within 5 to 10 minutes, so you'll need to keep track of the timer's time window or you'll be looking for current that's not supposed to be there.

Somewhere in the circuit there will be a relay to switch the high current necessary for the grid's operation. This may or may not be integral to the timer. A diagnostic procedure would be to jumper the relay's terminals to see if the relay is bad. You can either jump 12 volts to the relay's coil to make it pull in, or bypass the relay with a large-gauge jumper to see if the grid's wiring is intact between the relay and the window. A separate relay should be inexpensive and widely available, but if it's in the same package with the timer you'll pay as much as a hundred bucks.

Don't try to bypass the timer. Rear-window defrosters draw a substantial amount of current—10–20 amps, depending on the defroster. Most modern cars use a timer circuit to turn the grid off after a reasonable length of time. There are two reasons for this. The first is to reduce the electrical load on the alternator, which (especially during the wintertime) also supplies electricity for the headlights, heater fan, and windshield wipers. Couple that with the extra demands on the battery for starting in cold weather, and there may simply not be enough alternator capacity to keep the battery charged adequately. The second reason is simpler: The grid will overheat if it's left on too long. Imagine accidentally leaving it on during a long trip on a summer day. The heat from the grid added to the heat of the sun may crack the glass or contribute to deterioration of the window's rubber gaskets.

If you need to replace the timer or switch, you'll probably have to go to the car dealer for the parts.

NO HEAT

But let's say your grid has several lines that don't heat. You may find the break by simply inspecting the silk-screened grid along its length. This is easier on hatchbacks, minivans, and SUVs because you can open the back and look at the lines against the sky. Sedans require you to crawl into the back and poke your head into the area above the rear deck. Otherwise, you'll need to drag out the trusty DC voltmeter and hunt for it electrically.

Set your voltmeter for the 20-volt scale, and attach a couple of postage-stamp-size pieces of aluminum foil to the leads. This will prevent the probes from scratching the grid. You can simply lay the aluminum-foil tabs on the glass and press

lightly with one finger to make connection with the grid. If the window is large, it may help to have another pair of hands.

Start by measuring the voltage across the entire length of the grid. With the ignition on and the defroster turned on, you should see 12 volts on the meter with one tab at either end of the grid. Now move one tab to the center of the grid and measure again. The voltage should read 12 volts if the break is between the tabs, less if the break is outside the tabs. Similarly, measure the voltage on a grid line that is working properly, and you should see approximately 6 volts at the center, because you've just turned your defroster grid into a giant rheostat. By moving the tab along the damaged line, you'll see 12 volts on the meter until you reach the break, where the voltage will drop considerably all at once. This should allow you to pinpoint the break.

GRID REPAIR

Repairing the grid is simple. Many auto departments in large stores, and almost any dedicated auto parts store, can sell you a repair kit. Clean the area of the break with alcohol and a fresh, untinted paper towel. Don't use window cleaner, as it may leave a residue of wax or silicone. The kit will have an adhesive template to stick over the break, but you can use ordinary masking tape just as easily. The masking tape can be used to make a new line that exactly matches the width of your old grid, if the mask in the kit is too wide or narrow. Paint a stripe of the kit's conductive paint across the break. Allow it to dry for 10 to 15 minutes and remove the mask.

If you have several grid lines that are damaged, simply repeat the process. If the lines are damaged in more than one place along their length, you'll have to go back to step one and find the next break.

WORN DISC BRAKES

1

Remove the brake caliper.
With the car elevated and the wheel off, remove the brake caliper by taking out the caliper bolts with a socket wrench. Do not let the caliper hang freely or it could damage the connected brake line. Set the caliper on a raised surface instead.

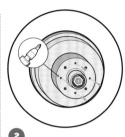

2

Replace the rotor.
When changing brake pads, you must either machine the rotors smooth or completely replace them to prevent them from unevenly wearing the new pads. Rotors aren't very expensive these days, so it's usually wise just to buy new ones.

3

Compress the piston.
The piston is the part of the caliper that applies the hydraulic pressure that presses the pads against the rotor, halting the wheels. Braking causes the piston to stick out slightly, so you'll need to compress the piston back into the caliper. With the old inner pad still in place, use a c-clamp to do this.

4

Reassemble the brake.
Snap your two new pads on both sides of the caliper and slide it back into position over the rotor. Then use a torque wrench to secure the caliper bolts to the manufacturer's torque specification, which can be found in your car's manual. Your local parts supplier would know, too, if the manual's gone missing.

Leaky Radiator

Crack a raw egg into the radiator filler cap (not the overflow tank, if you have one). The egg white will plug the hole—for a while. Now that you've fixed the hole in the radiator, you don't have enough water to refill it. Top off with diet soda (no sugar to gum up the water pump). Other liquids will work too, like recycled beer and that leftover iced tea.

▶ **OR TRY THIS!**
Dump in a small container of ground black pepper. The pepper won't dissolve but instead will remain in suspension. This allows it to temporarily plug minor leaks, buying you enough time to get to the shop.

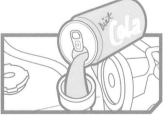

RUST

SURFACE RUST

Most surface rust happens when paint breaks down through mechanical or UV damage. Structurally, surface rust is not a problem, and, depending on the metal's thickness and alloy composition, a level of "passivation" may be reached. Regardless, it's best to correct surface rust as soon as you see it. The fix is not unlike general paint repair. Start by using an abrasive wheel or sandpaper **(1)** to cut through the paint and corrosion until clean, bright metal is visible. Next, apply primer, followed by paint **(2)**, then clear coat. Buff to blend the finishes **(3)**.

RUST BUBBLES

So you didn't correct the rust when it was limited to the surface, and now you've got a bubble. Molecules of rust are physically bigger than those of iron or steel. As a result, rust self-propagates by expanding and flaking away, exposing fresh base metal that begins corroding in turn. When rust penetrates into the surface it causes a rough, pitted type of damage called scale. Correcting scale means getting through the rust with a wire brush **(4)**, knocking down roughness with a grinding wheel, and attaining a smooth surface with sandpaper. Then apply a coat of primer and paint.

HOLES

Eventually, the base metal flakes away and leaves holes. Now you've got a bigger problem, and you've got two options. You can completely replace the affected panel (tough), or you can cut the rotten parts out and weld "patch panels" into place **(5)** (tougher). A rusted-through frame means the structural and crash integrity of the car is questionable, and it should be inspected and repaired by a qualified repair facility.

SQUEAKY SERPENTINE BELT

Most modern cars don't use old-fashioned V-belts anymore. Instead, a single belt, winding its way through a forest of pulleys, can now drive every single engine accessory at the same time. A single belt only an inch or so wide saves 3 or 4 inches of engine room real estate. Better still: Most of the serpentine-belt installations use a spring-loaded tensioner pulley that keeps a constant preload on the belt, eliminating the need to adjust the tension. Plus, serpentine belts don't wear out, at least not for a really long time. A fresh belt will probably last 150,000 miles without any maintenance at all.

A squealing noise is indicative of a problem, but might not require replacement of the belt. Misaligned pulleys or a seized tensioner or idler pulley can generate some noise as well. A belt that's starting to disintegrate will show damage to the ribs or cords, which can usually be seen without dismantling anything. But you might need a flashlight and a dental mirror to see the fraying or cracking.

FRESH BELT

Start by studying the old belt's routing, which should be easy if the belt is still in place. If the belt is wadded up, don't worry: There should be a belt-routing placard under the hood. Otherwise, look in the owner's manual. Most cars provide a common ⅜-inch-square hole in the tensioner's arm to release the tensioner. Simply use a ratchet to loosen the belt, and unthread it from the pulleys.

Inspect the belt for damage. Cracks across the ribs are the most common indication of a belt that's simply at the end of its life span. Little rubber bands of rib, tufts of fiberglass-reinforcing belt, or disintegrating belt edges are indications of a problem with the pulleys, idlers, or tensioners. A high-mileage belt that's just looking worn can simply be replaced. If there are other indications of damage from misalignment, get out the straightedge and make note of what isn't square.

A bent accessory-mounting bracket can make a pulley crooked, and you'll need to realign it. A steel bracket could be bent back into place, but a couple of shim washers might be

An ordinary ⅜-inch extension and ratchet is used to unload the tensioner. Then you can unthread the belt from around the pulleys.

We used thread-locking compound to seal the new bolt that was provided with the tensioner.

Use a straight-edge to see if all the pulleys are coplanar and square. If they're not, the new belt won't last long.

Torque the new tensioner to the specified degree of tightness. Yes, that means with a torque wrench, not your carefully calibrated elbow.

The hash mark on the body of the tensioner should fall between the high and low tension marks when the new belt is installed.

a better option. If you're replacing a belt because of a fried alternator or a seized a/c compressor, don't assume the new accessory or bracket will run true, either.

The pulley should freewheel smoothly. The spring should have an appropriate amount of tension (which you can check with a belt tension gauge once the belt is installed), and there should be no friction in the pivot. Tensioner assemblies are usually not very expensive. It's the same for any idler pulleys, which should spin freely.

Is the area where the belt lives oily? Engine oil will rapidly degrade the rubber in the belt. Repair any leaky engine seals, like the crankshaft or camshaft front seal, or any gaskets—lest the new belt should go south in short order. Clean up any old oil, too.

Check all the pulleys as well. Old rubber or dirt can build up in the bottom of the pulley grooves. You may need to clean the grooves with brake cleaner or a wire brush to remove any debris.

BUTTONING UP

To install a new tensioner and reinstall the belt, hold the tensioner slack with one hand as you thread the last pulley. Once the belt's in place, start the engine and let it idle for a minute or two. Check the belt tension by looking at the tensioner arm—the mark cast into the tensioner body will fall between the high and low marks if the belt is the correct part number and is installed properly. If you removed any of the radiator shrouding to access the belt, don't neglect to reinstall it once you've finished. You certainly don't want any new noises coming from under the hood.

Leaking Gas Tank

Stuff a wedge from a bar of soap in the hole. It'll last long enough to get to town. Or just a few hundred yards past that stream you need to ford.

THE REARVIEW MIRROR FELL OFF

Most vehicles rely on a simple glue joint to hold the rearview mirror onto the windshield. Your first step is to pick up a rearview mirror installation kit from an auto parts store. Don't buy one that's hanging on a hook from your local odd-lot-merchandise emporium or any other place that isn't likely to have a fresh kit on hand. These kits have a limited shelf life, especially if not stored properly. Similarly, don't buy one and keep it stashed in your hot glove box—it won't last.

Park your car in a place where the temperature is somewhere between 50°F and 75° F. Park in the shade, because if the glass is too hot, the adhesive will set with less strength. Rainy days will leave moisture on the glass.

Remove the metal button from the mirror assembly **(1)**. Very few (usually older) vehicles have mirrors that glue directly to the glass, but most will have a button you glue on first and then attach the mirror to. Very important: Find some

way to label the button THIS SIDE UP. The last thing you need is to glue on the button upside down. Mark it with a felt pen or a scratch at the very top or bottom. Don't mark the side that faces the glass, because the next thing we're going to do with the button is clean that surface down to bare metal.

There are probably some remnants of the glue on the windshield. Before you clean anything up, use a felt pen, grease pencil, or a piece of masking tape to mark the position of the button **(2)**. Mark the outside of the glass. Don't forget that there might be wires to connect if you have any electrical components in the mirror.

Remove every last vestige of old adhesive from the button. If there is any adhesive left on the glass, scrape it off with a single-edge razor blade. Follow up with some solvent, such as lacquer thinner or rubbing alcohol **(3)**, to remove your fingerprints from both the glass and the

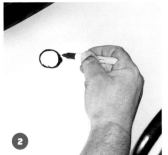

and squeeze a single, generous drop out onto the face of the button **(4)**. Press the button onto the glass **(5)**. You get only one chance, so aim precisely. Hold the button in place for 1 minute, using moderate pressure (even if the directions in the kit say 10 seconds).

Now it's a simple matter of reinstalling the mirror. If you have a setscrew-style attachment, it's easy. Just hold the mirror in place with one hand

button. With the car and glass at a moderate temperature—and the button right side up—open the small vial of adhesive with a razor blade while you run the setscrew in with the other. Use just enough torque on the wrench to keep the mirror from rattling.

Cracked Dashboard

Cut out the damage.
Use a razor blade to cut a border around the damaged plastic or vinyl, then peel or rip it off, along with any other areas on the dash that feel brittle. To check for brittleness, press your thumb into the dash. If the vinyl feels hard or cracks, it's no good.

Fill the crack.
Next, spray some 3M Polyolefin Adhesion Promoter on the exposed foam rubber. Then apply a thin layer of 3M EZ Sand Flexible Parts Repair, an epoxy that dries like hard plastic. Cover the entire hole and a bit of the surrounding plastic with a thin layer. Once the EZ Sand is dry (the label should specify the required time), sand it even with the rest of the dash, using 320- or 400-grit sandpaper. The patch will be thin. Be careful not to create holes.

Apply texture and color.
If you're repairing a large part of the dash in a basic color like black, you could use a textured paint or even bed liner to cover the damaged area. Both mimic the surface feel of vinyl. For a smaller or more colorful fix, spray a layer of black SEM Texture Coating paint over the sanded area to duplicate the original texture. When dry, apply a coat of SEM Color Coat in the same color as your dash.

STUCK FASTENER

One of a mechanic's biggest stumbling blocks can be removing stuck fasteners. First, you have to bring a tool to bear with enough torque to unfreeze the fastener, more than was used years ago to install that nut or bolt. If you can't loosen the fastener with sheer strength, reach for a torch. Iron oxide—rust—is larger than the steel it was created from, and the extra volume locks the two parts together like Super Glue. Heat, cool; heat, cool; add some penetrating oil and eventually you'll get the rust to crumble to powder and your nuts will loosen up.

▶ Or try a can of Loctite Freeze & Release, which accomplishes the same thing with a blast of cold—really cold—penetrating oil. Just don't frostbite your fingers.

SQUEAKY
BRAKES

Let's make one thing clear right up front: Sometimes your brakes will make noise. If you expect supreme silence, or expect your mechanic to make your brakes totally mute in every circumstance—that just may not be possible. Relax, don't worry. A squeaking brake can stop a vehicle as quickly as a quiet one.

So what makes the squeal, then? Modern brakes use a cast-iron disc, squeezed between two brake pads lined with friction material. Under the right conditions, the disc, the pads, and the caliper they're mounted in can start to vibrate—in exactly the same way a violin's string vibrates when stroked by the horsehairs on a bow. The violin's pitch is controlled by the position of the violinist's finger on the string, not by how hard or how fast the bow is stroked. Similarly, most brake squeals occur at a single discrete frequency. The speed of the vehicle and how hard you press down on the left pedal will only change the volume of noise, because the pitch is controlled by the stiffness and mass of the pad and disc.

Inadequate development at the manufacturer that leaves brake systems prone to noise can usually be overcome by a Saturday mechanic without totally reengineering the caliper/mount/pad/disc system. We can try to damp out the noise, or simply change the resonant frequency of the whole arrangement until it stops singing in any audible frequency. Here's how.

NORMAL PAD NOISES

Many brake pad compositions will make a swishing or grinding noise for the first few stops in the morning until the pads warm up and drive off any moisture they've accumulated overnight. Ever notice a hissing or grinding noise on some rainy or dewy mornings? It's the pads sweeping a thin film of rust that's formed on the iron discs, and it's perfectly normal.

In the past, brake pad friction material relied heavily on asbestos. Unfortunately, asbestos tended to give asbestos workers and brake mechanics lung cancer, so the industry has almost completely changed over to less dangerous alternatives. Kevlar is one material that's seen a lot of use, but it tends to be dusty. Improved brake performance is more important nowadays because of increased safety requirements and equipment—and the extra road-hugging weight that comes along with these. That leads to the increased use of metallics and ceramics in the brake pad friction material. And this stuff can make the brakes hiss or even grind a little as you slow down. It's a small price to pay for increased performance. So all pad noise is fine, right? Hold up there, Sparky, there's one brake noise you need to pay attention to right away. Many brake pads have a small finger of spring steel that will scrape on the disc as the pad reaches its wear limit. This tells you that it's time to change pads for fresh, thicker ones before the friction material wears completely away, and you're trying to slow down on the metal backing plates. It's a sound not easily confused with brake squeal—it's more of a ripping-sheet-metal noise, not a single, high-pitched note.

HOW TO SILENCE THE NOISE

One fix is to simply change pads to a different type of friction material. It's usually hard to

This is one product we've tried that usually works to bond brake pads to the caliper and reduce or eliminate squeal.

This sheet-metal finger is just long enough to contact the disc when the pads are mostly worn out. The noise is calculated to make you replace the pads.

Here are two different compositions of brake pads. The one on the left is the stock pad installed by the factory, with a high concentration of organic fibers and brass particles. The aftermarket pad uses less brass and more ceramics for longer wear and improved braking.

beat the original-equipment pads for a good compromise of pad life, noise, grip, dust creation, and price, but changing to an aftermarket premium metallic or ceramic pad just might change the interaction that affects the resonant frequency of the pad and disc and, literally, change its tune.

Go into any auto parts store and you'll see a shelf full of potions and widgets claiming to cure squeaks. Be leery of simple aerosols that you spray onto the pad's friction material. It's not a good idea to try anything that changes the friction characteristics of the pad. The first reason your brake system exists is, in fact, to make your car slow down. Anything that could reduce that system's effectiveness in any way is probably not a good idea.

Still got noise? Or still have plenty of pad material remaining and don't want to drop fifty or a hundred bucks on a fresh set? You may be able to decouple the piston acoustically from the pad by purchasing shims made of Teflon, which are intended to go between the pad and the caliper's hydraulic piston. Shims sometimes work and sometimes they don't. Warning: Some calipers will not have enough extra travel in the piston bore to allow any shimming without making the brakes drag, at least with fresh, unworn pads.

You can achieve a similar decoupling without Teflon shims by simply coating the back face of the pad's backing plates with high-temp brake grease or even antiseize compound. Unlike shims, this tweak won't last forever, as water and road dirt will wash it away eventually.

We chose high-end, ceramic-based pads for our brake job, hoping the different friction characteristics would cure the squeal. Surprise: The new pads came out of the box fitted with Teflon-coated shims already installed.

TAKE ADVANTAGE OF THE BACKING PLATE

Instead of using shims or lubricants to decouple the pad from the caliper, stick the backing plate to the piston or caliper housing, effectively making its mass far larger. That will move the system's resonant frequency out of the squealing range. A smear of Super Glue won't do it: You need something that will withstand the water, salt, filth, and especially the heat that cars see every day. How hot do brake systems get? Brake discs can glow bright orange at the bottom of Pikes Peak, and flames have been known to shoot out of the brake drums of trucks descending Donner Pass. After a few hot laps in a race car, the brakes can visibly glow.

Most products are basically anaerobic adhesives, applied as either a lipstick-style film or a toothpaste-style goo. Remove and clean up the old pads, or use new pads. Clean the area on the piston and caliper where the pad backing plate touches. Apply the antisqueal adhesive, reinstall the pads, and button up. These anaerobic products will stay gummy until you apply the brakes and squeeze out the oxygen. Then they stick like, well, glue.

Whenever you're installing any brake parts, be sure you remove any corrosion or road dirt from the mating parts—the brake pad or caliper housing needs to be able to slide in and out to compensate for wear. Clean up any sliding parts, which may require a wire brush or a file, until you can push the pads in and out with your bare hands. Replace any brake hardware (especially on drum brakes) that isn't in perfect condition—hey, it's cheap insurance. Apply a thin film of high-temp brake grease to any sliding surfaces. Obviously, avoid getting anything like grease or antiseize compound on the pad or disc, and clean any greasy handprints off the disc surface before you hang the wheel on, too.

When installing new or old pads, sparingly coat all the sliding surfaces on the pads, pins, and hardware with high-temp brake grease. Use sparingly, and—duh—don't get any on the pads or discs.

File, sandpaper, or grind any burrs, extra paint, rust, or high spots off the pads, new or old, to be sure the pad will slide easily in and out as the brakes are applied and released.

Check out the raised areas—leftovers from the manufacturing process. We had to file down the steel backing plate on this aftermarket pad.

HOW TO BLEED YOUR BRAKES

Air in the brake system can make your brake pedal feel spongy and vague. You should flush the fluid every two or three years, but it can be a moderately difficult DIY repair.

WHY IT'S HAPPENING

Because air is compressible, when an air bubble or three get pumped into the brake lines, you have the equivalent of a very soft spring in the solid column of brake fluid between your foot and the wheels. Bleeding the brakes will flush that air out.

The job also involves replacing the old fluid with fresh, which is a good thing. Why would the fluid need to be replaced? It becomes contaminated with atmospheric dirt and abrasive metal wear particles from moving parts in the master cylinder and calipers. It absorbs moisture from the air, which can lower the boiling point of the fluid enough to make it boil at the end of a long downhill grade. (And steam, like air, is compressible.) High temperatures from those high-energy-dissipation stops can degrade the alcohol-based fluid itself. Eventually, your water-clear brake fluid starts to look more like squid ink.

Antilock braking systems are even less tolerant of contaminated fluid and air than non-ABS. The ABS hydraulic pump operates at several thousand psi, forcing brake fluid through very small valves. This can whip air and brake fluid into something like the foam on a latte, which makes bleeding difficult. Those same valves and pump can easily be damaged by tiny abrasive particles.

The good news: Air that has entered the ABS controller can be bled out. Bad news: Some vehicles require the use of a hideously expensive proprietary ABS scan tool to cycle the pump and valves to purge the last of the air. But there's a simple solution to that: Never let any air enter the system. You can flush a system with fresh fluid by using nothing more than a wrench that fits the bleeder bolts and a helper.

HOW TO FIX IT

To properly bleed the brakes, start with a couple of 8-ounce cans of fresh brake fluid. An unopened can has a long shelf life. An opened can should be discarded within a few weeks. Get the vehicle up in the air and remove all four wheels. Your next task is to make sure the bleeder valves can be loosened. You'll need a box wrench that fits the bleeder bolt. A crescent wrench or Vise-Grip probably will just round off the bolt's flats. A little penetrating oil drizzled on the bolts the day before will help. So will some judicious tapping with a hammer to break up any corrosion. Loosen the bolts, but leave them closed.

If you can't turn the bleeders without breaking them off, you'll need to replace the brake calipers or wheel cylinders. See the above notation about penetrating oil and light hammer taps before applying enough torque to break these minuscule, hollow bolts.

Sneak into the kitchen and appropriate the small turkey baster. Remove the top of the master cylinder reservoir and suck out as much of the

Suck the old fluid and sediment out of the master cylinder reservoir with a turkey baster or syringe.

Top off the reservoir with fresh fluid as you bleed the system. Don't let it get more than half empty.

old squid ink as you can. Clean any sediment out of the reservoir with a clean, lint-free rag. Do not spill any brake fluid on any painted surfaces. It will remove the paint pretty much immediately.

Get a piece of clear plastic tubing (aquarium tubing is fine, and it's cheap). Push one end of the tube over the brake bleeder bolt at the right rear of the car. Put the other end of the tube into a small, clear bottle with an inch or two of clean brake fluid in it. (This will keep air from being sucked back into the brake cylinder or caliper.) Put a piece of 1 × 4 lumber or some other spacer under the pedal to prevent the pedal from traveling too far when line pressure is released. Top off the master cylinder reservoir with fresh fluid and put the cover back on the reservoir. Fluid will squirt out of an open reservoir every time the pedal is released.

TIME FOR HELP

Have a helper sit in the driver's seat and await your orders. Here's the drill: You say "down."

He or she depresses the brake pedal with about the same amount of force needed to keep the car from rolling forward at a traffic light. Then your helper says "down" and keeps the pressure on. When you hear the call, warn your helper that the brake pedal is about to sink underfoot and to keep the pressure on constantly. Then crack the bleeder bolt a quarter-turn. Some of the old, contaminated fluid will trickle down the tubing into your bottle. When the trickle stops, close the bleeder. Then you say "up." Your helper says "up," and removes his or her foot from the pedal.

Repeat this process until fresh, clear fluid comes from the bleeder. Any out-of-sequence moves can suck air into the caliper. Yes, the end of the tubing is submerged in fluid, but air can travel past the threads on the bleeder bolt into the caliper if there's ever any negative pressure in the system while the bleeder is cracked.

Every half-dozen or so iterations, top off the reservoir with fresh fluid. Do not allow the reservoir to get more than half empty—air can be sucked into the master cylinder unless the fluid level remains well above the bottom of the reservoir that feeds the cylinder. Once clean fluid is coming out of the brake, snug the bleeder bolt, move your operation to the left rear wheel, and start all over again. Next, repeat the process with the right front wheel and finally with the left front wheel . Follow that with a few strokes of fresh fluid from all four, again. Don't forget to keep the reservoir topped off.

A bleeder bolt can become difficult to remove. Use a proper-fitting box wrench to keep from rounding it off.

Got ABS? You may need to use a scan tool during the bleeding process to cycle the pump and valves.

DRIVEWAY
STAINS

If you do your own work on your car or other equipment, you're bound to have oil stains on your garage floor or driveway. Here's something that works and is basically free: ground-up drywall. Pulverize a small piece with a hammer, then grind it up in your hands and sprinkle it over the stains. Let it stay in place overnight before rinsing it off. If the first application doesn't remove the whole stain, try it again. Some very old stains can take three or more applications.

DEAD HORN

If your horn blows for a few seconds but at a reduced volume, this at least means that the circuitry that f,eeds the horn is alive and well. Most vehicles actually have two horns, wired to sound at the same time. They usually will be of a different pitch, sounding a chord instead of a single note. Some luxury cars use three horns for a more melodious sound. The horns generally are mounted to the radiator core support or somewhere behind the vehicle's grille. A cursory rooting around in the engine compartment should locate them.

If one or more horns are inoperative, the sound will be slightly reduced and less pleasant. If you suspect one of your horns isn't sounding, have a helper depress the horn button briefly (ignition on) while you touch the suspected horn with your fingers. (We recommend earplugs.) No sound? Remove the wiring connector, clean up the spade lugs, and then reinstall them. Still nothing? If the horn has only one wire running to it, it relies on its mounting bolt to complete the circuit to ground. Unbolt the horn, clean up any corrosion and reinstall it.

If there's still no sound, make sure the horn is actually the problem by running a jumper wire directly to the battery terminals. If one horn is defunct, replace it. Generally, the horn will have an imprint or a sticker identifying it as a HIGH or LOW tone. To preserve the OEM horn character, you'll need an exact replacement. This will ensure that the horn's pitch will be the same. If you're not fussy, any universal replacement will work, although you may have to adapt the mounting.

But what if your horns don't make any sound at all? Then the problem lies elsewhere in the wiring. Now's the time to check the fuse, which probably is buried in the bottom of the dashboard, in the driver's kick panel, or under the hood—or almost anywhere on the front half of the vehicle if it's not in one of those obvious places. Check the owner's manual for the location of the fuse box and of the specific fuse. If it looks like the metal strip inside the fuse has failed, replace it with one of the same amperage rating. Once in a blue moon, fuses will seem to fail for no apparent reason. If the fuse is bad, odds are you've got a problem that will make it blow again, sooner or later.

With a good fuse, you'll need a 12-volt test light or a voltmeter. You also should find a shop manual or, at the very least, a schematic diagram of the horn circuit. Start by testing for 12 volts at the connector to the horn. One side of the circuit is carried by the car's metal frame, so you'll need to check between a good ground point and the wiring connector for the horn. If there's no voltage at the connector, try checking the horn relay.

The horn relay switches a large current to the horns at a signal from the low-current horn button in the steering wheel. It's a simple, inexpensive, single-pole single-throw (SPST) relay, packaged in a small metal or plastic box with five spade-lug connectors. If you're unlucky, your vehicle uses a relay that's integrated into a larger box of sparks that also controls several other functions on your car, such as the headlights or the turn signals. This part is considerably more expensive. Consult the shop manual for the location of the relay, as it will not necessarily be near the fuse box. A simple SPST relay will have a constant supply of 12 volts to it, a lead that runs through the harness to the horn, another lead that runs to the horn switch in the wheel, and a ground. Check that voltage is coming into the relay and leaving it when the switch is pushed. If it's not, try grounding the lead that goes to the horn button to make the relay pull in. If the horn sounds, the relay is good but the horn button or its wiring is bad. You may be able to simply replace the relay if that's the problem. Otherwise, you'll need to do some serious detective work to chase down the open circuit.

The horn button (or buttons) is generally attached to the top of the airbag shroud. To be safe and avoid accidentally setting off the airbag, get a trained technician to remove the airbag for you and then reinstall it after your horn has been fixed. He can test the airbag system to be sure it will go off when it's supposed to and not go off when it's not. The airbag must be removed to access the slip rings or the clock spring that carries voltage up the rotating steering column from the relay to the horn button. If you need to access this, leave the job to a service technician who has training and service manuals detailing the correct procedures. Incidentally, a horn that intermittently blows on its own generally is caused by a bad clock spring that shorts out to ground randomly.

THE GUIDE TO CAR WOBBLES

Cars, like animals, can communicate with people when something's wrong. Often it's through a really annoying, odd noise. Sometimes, though, it's a feeling—perhaps a subtle one. But if there's a worn or unbalanced component, the most sophisticated car rides like a road-going Tilt-A-Whirl. How and when the problem manifests itself helps pinpoint the source. Here are the most common causes of those unsettling sensations.

What you feel: The steering wheel shakes in your hands and the entire car vibrates, as though you're driving atop railroad ties.
What it is: At least one wheel is bent, most likely from hitting a curb or pothole while going a little too fast. Steel wheels are more prone to bending than the more expensive alloy ones. Alloy wheels tend to crack or break, rather than simply bending.
What to do: Replace the wheel and have the tire checked by a professional for internal damage.

What you feel: A regular but low click or cluck that becomes a steady vibration through the pedals and steering wheel in a front-wheel drive vehicle, and through the seat in a rear-wheel drive.
What it is: A worn constant velocity (CV) joint on a front-wheel drive, or a universal joint on a rear-wheel drive. Although these joints should last the life of the car, the grease may leak out over time.
What to do: Replace the joints.

What you feel: The steering wheel shakes at all speeds. When you steer, the car is slow to respond and its response is not accurate.
What it is: A wheel is loose. Too many auto repair techs rely on their air wrenches when mounting tires. If the nuts are overtorqued, the stud threads may get stripped or even break.
What to do: Check every wheel nut. Tighten them all to spec with a torque wrench, moving the wrench in a crisscross pattern.

What you feel: A sometimes bone-shuddering vibration that's in sync with engine—not road—speed.
What it is: An engine misfire due to wet spark plug wires or connections, a fouled fuel injector, or something worse—a bent or burned valve. If it happens only in wet weather, bet on an ignition problem.
What to do: The CHECK ENGINE light will come on in modern cars and trucks. A scan tool will reveal the root cause.

5

What you feel: The steering wheel shakes, at times violently, at a certain speed range. Faster or slower, and everything's fine.

What it is: A front-tire balance weight is gone. You can spot missing balance weights in a weekly walk-around before driving. (The inspection may also turn up an underinflated tire, a broken lens or a burned-out bulb—not to mention dings and scratches that weren't there yesterday.)

What to do: Have all four tires rebalanced.

6

What you feel: The body is seemingly disconnected from the wheels. It floats eerily over rises but lands hard after driving over potholes and speed bumps, and it continues to rise and fall after you stop.

What it is: Worn shock absorbers or strut cartridges. The ride and handling will gradually deteriorate before the shocks are shot. Regular driving over broken tar, or off-road, accelerates degradation.

What to do: Replace them all or, at the very least, both rears or both fronts, as necessary.

7

What you feel: The steering wheel seems detached from the front wheels. The car won't track around long sweeping turns. This is accompanied by odd clanks and thumps from somewhere up front.

What it is: Worn tie-rod ends or ball joints. Or both. Torn or cracked rubber boots allow the grease to escape, which accelerates wear.

What to do: Replace them with ones that have grease fittings, and keep them lubricated. You'll need a front-end alignment, too.

8

What you feel: The brake pedal pulses steadily as you step on it.

What it is: A brake rotor or drum is warped, probably due to overheating from hard use or from over-tightened wheel nuts. Since a vehicle's weight shifts toward the front under braking, the front brakes do the lion's share of the slowing and stopping and, therefore, wear more quickly than the rear ones.

What to do: Change the brake rotor and pads. While you're at it, check the calipers; replace if necessary.

STUCK WIPER BLADE

First things first: Check the fuse. A wiper assembly that refuses to move might have a simple blown fuse. But usually fuses don't blow on their own. Even at full stall, the current draw of the motor should be well below the fuse's rating. If the fuse is blown, odds are there's something else wrong, like a shorted wiper-motor armature or faulty wiring anywhere along the harness between the motor and the switch. Even a mechanical problem like a seized bushing can make a fuse eventually fail.

The fuse is okay, or you've replaced it with one that has the appropriate amp rating. There's still no action? With the wipers and ignition on, whack the motor assembly with the handle of a screwdriver or a rubber mallet. If that gets things moving, you've got a bad commutator or an open winding on the armature. When the motor parks, if the brushes are sitting on the bad segment, no current flows. Whacking the whole business smartly can sometimes jolt things into motion. Because there are often a dozen windings on the armature, the motor runs fine until the next time it comes to rest on the bad spot.

MECHANICALS

The mechanism on windshield wipers is as simple as could be. Inside that gearbox on the motor is a simple worm gear, spinning a ring gear and bellcrank that translate the motor's circular motion to a linear one, back and forth. Simple joints attach the transmission arms to the wiper pivot shaft, which is fixed to the cowl by some sort of pillow block. Lack of lubrication, ice buildup, or simple corrosion takes its toll and can slow things down. A loose joint will leave lost motion, which can cause the blades to either flop around or, worse

yet, catch each other and get tangled. The bad news: Sometimes it's difficult to access the area under the cowl. Worse news: If you go to the trouble of buying an aftermarket service manual in the hope that it will provide some guidance—any guidance—as to how to remove the cowl, it probably won't. Cars are complicated enough that not every single thing that needs to be taken apart can be fit into a bound book, and straightforward stuff like bodywork often fails to make the cut. (Think about it: Is it ultimately more important to know the torque values for the connecting-rod bolts or where all the screws to the cowl are hidden?)

A favorite friction point is the bearing surface between the wiper shaft and its mounting block, which is often nothing more than a steel shaft running through a hole cast in plastic. A corroded steel shaft can swell up and bind. It's not a bad idea to dismantle the mechanism, wire-brush off any corrosion, and reassemble the whole thing with a generous dollop of silicone grease.

Disintegrating rubber mounting blocks and crumbling nylon bushings can leave slop in the linkage or cause excess friction that makes the wipers run as though they're coated with molasses. There's no recourse but to replace these. Unfortunately, some of these parts have no part number from the dealer, requiring you to replace an entire expensive assembly—or improvise. We bought a transmission arm, complete with bearing block and pivot, at NAPA for a fifth of what the dealer wanted.

MOTOR WOES

Is that motor assembly bad? Before you trot out and spend money on a new one, there are a few things to check out. Get a schematic diagram for the wiper system and parse out how it works. Generally, there are a couple of different windings on the motor for high- and low-speed operation. These will be supplied, respectively, with 12 volts when the ignition is on and the wiper switch is in, duh, high or low. Start by back-probing the connector to the motor to see if the 12 volts are making it that far. If so, pull the connector off and look for corrosion on the terminals. Check the park wire as well.

Got voltage? You might have a wiper system that switches the ground side of the circuit on and off. In that case you'll see voltage everywhere, even when the wipers are turned off. . . . Back to the schematic.

As a last-resort diagnostic, jumper 12 volts directly from the battery to the appropriate pin on the motor's power connector. If there's still no sign of life, it's time for a new motor. Before you

unbolt the old motor, detach the transmission linkage, which may have nice, plastic ball-and-socket joints, simple pins with nylon bushings and E-rings, or some other arcane method of carrying the motion across the car to both wiper arms.

PUTTING IT ALL TOGETHER

Reassembly should be straightforward. Lubricate all moving parts, using silicone grease on rubber pieces. (Avoid using petroleum-based grease on rubber parts—it will deteriorate them.)

Some wiper arms have a friction fit to the wiper post. To position the arms correctly, briefly cycle the power to the wipers to park them. Now attach the arms in their correct at-rest position. Other wipers have splines that mate in only one position, so if the arms don't rest properly when parked, you'll need to adjust the linkage elsewhere, probably at the middle pivots.

Removing the cowl trim might make it easier to access the wiper transmission. A fingerful of white grease on all the moving parts is a must. Check for sloppy fit and lost motion. Lube the pivot points as well.

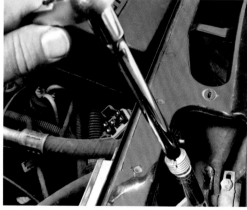

On this truck, the resting position of the wipers on the windshield is trimmed out by loosening the transmission arm and sliding the pivot left and right, because the arm only indexes on the shaft in one position.

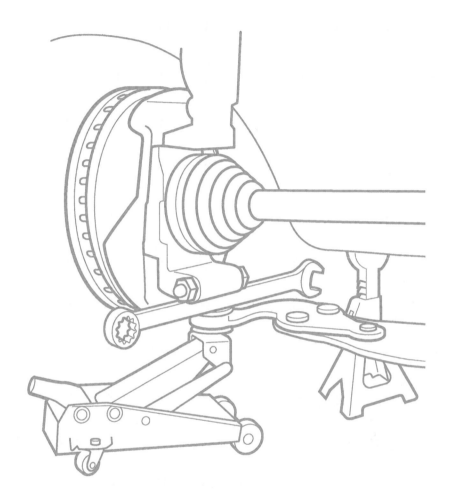

STUCK BALL JOINT

Freeing front-suspension ball joints can be frustrating. Rather than wrestling with crowbars and special tools, jack up the corner of the car and lower it safely onto a jackstand placed under the frame. Reposition the hydraulic jack under the suspension and raise it until the car nearly lifts off the stand. Take your largest wrench and wedge it between the bottom of the steering knuckle and the suspension arm. Lower the jack to force the suspension geometry to press the joint loose. If this doesn't work, the wrench is great to hammer away on.

YARD

CHAPTER 03

Lawn Pests

Insecticides tend to kill anything that lives in your soil, even good guys like earthworms. This year, try nematodes, microscopic worms that prey only on offending pests. Arbico Organic's five varieties ($43 to treat 3,200 square feet) attack fleas, ticks, grubs, and nearly anything else. To use, identify the right nematodes for your pests. Mix them with water and apply to problem areas with a watering can.

DEAD SPOTS
IN THE LAWN

When disease gets a foothold in your lawn you need to take immediate action. Bag your clippings and don't put them in your compost pile. Avoid walking through infected turf, especially when it's wet. And follow these instructions.

SUMMER DISEASES

If you find dark grass that looks water-soaked and then develops into browned-out, circular areas, you could be looking at brown patch—a condition prevalent during moist, hot weather on overfertilized lawns. The patches can be several inches to several feet in diameter, with some green leaves persisting and roots remaining intact. Grass blades may have irregular ash-gray lesions that run along one side and are bordered by a dark-brown margin. Management includes using cultivars, such as the ryegrasses Pennant and Prelude, America bluegrass, and slow-release nitrogen fertilizer. Water deeply but infrequently, mow high, remove excess thatch, and improve aeration and drainage.

Low-nitrogen lawns—especially those stressed by drought and heavy dew—are candidates for dollar spot. On taller lawns you'll find mottled, straw-colored, 4- to 6-inch-diameter patches. Grass blades will show light tan bands bounded by reddish-brown margins. Patches may merge to form large, irregular areas, and grayish-white mycelium may be present in early morning. Overseed with a blend of improved cultivars, such as Adelphi, the perennial ryegrass All Star, and Reliant fescue. Maintain adequate nitrogen and potassium fertility, water deeply when necessary, and remove excess thatch. If your lawn is prone to dollar spot, remove the morning dew by dragging a hose across the lawn.

Pythium blight spreads rapidly and involves the entire grass plant. It occurs on poorly drained soils with a wet grass canopy, and when nighttime temperature plus relative humidity equals 150. Symptoms include 1- to 6-inch-diameter brown, wilted patches that turn to streaks, indicating drainage patterns. In early morning, the grass is slimy, dark, and matted. White, cottony mycelium may be present when grass is wet. As it dries, the grass turns light tan and shrivels. To fight the problem, improve drainage, don't overwater, aerate, reduce excess thatch, and avoid nitrogen fertilizer during warm weather. Check calcium levels and add lime if necessary.

Slow, hot-weather growth on compacted, shady lawns with low fertility are ingredients for a condition known as rust. It's characterized by small yellow flecks that develop into pustules, releasing yellow, orange, red, or dark-brown spores. From a distance, the turf appears orange or yellow, and spore residue rubs off if touched. Treat it with rust-resistant cultivars of fine fescues and the Kentucky bluegrasses Challenger and Eclipse. Provide appropriate fertilization and irrigation, prune to reduce shade, maintain aeration, and mow frequently, bagging clippings.

SPRING TO FALL DISEASES

One common condition that's caused by over 50 varieties of fungi is characterized by rings of dark green grass. Called fairy rings, these areas may be accompanied by mushrooms, while midsummer and fall rings are more apt to be composed of dead grass. Fairy rings are difficult to eradicate unless dug out to a depth of at least 1 foot. Aerating to improve water penetration and fertilizing to minimize color variation are helpful.

Stripe smut appears in cool weather, causing yellow, stunted growth in 6- to 12-inch-diameter patches. You'll recognize it by black stripes of erupted spores along grass blades, which later dry and become shredded and curled. The best defense is to use cultivars, such as the bluegrasses Adelphi or Midnight, and maintain adequate fertilization. When the disease is present, water thoroughly, mow often, and bag clippings.

If you find 6- to 12-inch circular patches of matted, straw-colored grass surrounding a tuft of green grass, this may be necrotic ring spot. You may also notice that the thatch in the affected area has decomposed, creating a sunken appearance. This disease is especially common to bluegrass and red fescue. While the fungus is active during cool, moist periods, the damage frequently doesn't show itself until later, when turf is stressed. Overseed with disease-resistant cultivars of tall fescue and perennial ryegrasses, such as Classic and Eclipse, or Columbia bluegrass. Water to lessen drought and heat stress, and avoid excessive fertilizer use. Remove excess thatch and maintain adequate aeration and drainage.

Helminthosporium melting out and leaf spot are two phases of a fungal disease that is especially destructive on overfertilized, lush bluegrasses. The initial phase, stimulated by cloudy, moist weather in the 70°F–85°F range, displays distinctive dark purple spots that develop into buff-colored oval lesions, bordered by a dark brown or purple margin. The color of the blades turns yellow and then tan. During the melting-out phase, rot develops in roots and crowns. To handle the condition, use resistant bluegrass cultivars, such as Glade, Nugget, or Pennstar. Avoid excessive use of nitrogen fertilizer, water infrequently but deeply, mow high, aerate, top-dress with organic mulch, and remove excess thatch.

FALL TO SPRING DISEASES

Gray snow mold (typhula blight) is strictly a cold-weather disease, appearing where snow has melted, especially in areas where there have been piles of snow or drifts. Its symptoms include irregular 2- to 24-inch-diameter patches of bleached-out, matted turf, covered with moldy, grayish-white mycelium. Tiny black or orange-brown spherical sclerotia (hard fungus bodies) may be embedded in the leaves and crowns of infected plants. To handle this problem, avoid late, heavy nitrogen fertilization in the fall. Keep thatch to a minimum and the height of your grass lower going into winter. Avoid piling snow onto your lawn, and prevent compaction by limiting activity when the ground is covered with snow. In the spring you'll want to rake early to promote drying and to reduce matting. If you notice any damage at that time, fertilize lightly.

Pink snow mold (fusarium patch) develops in cool, moist, cloudy weather, with or without snow cover. It's distinguished by small, light-tan to rusty-brown circular patches up to 2 feet in diameter that become ringlike as interior grass regrows. When the area is moist, salmon-colored mycelium is visible in sunlight. Treatment includes late fall fertilization with slow-release nitrogen fertilizer. Keep thatch low and don't allow leaves or debris to remain on the lawn over the winter. Rake in early spring, followed by light fertilization if the lawn shows damage.

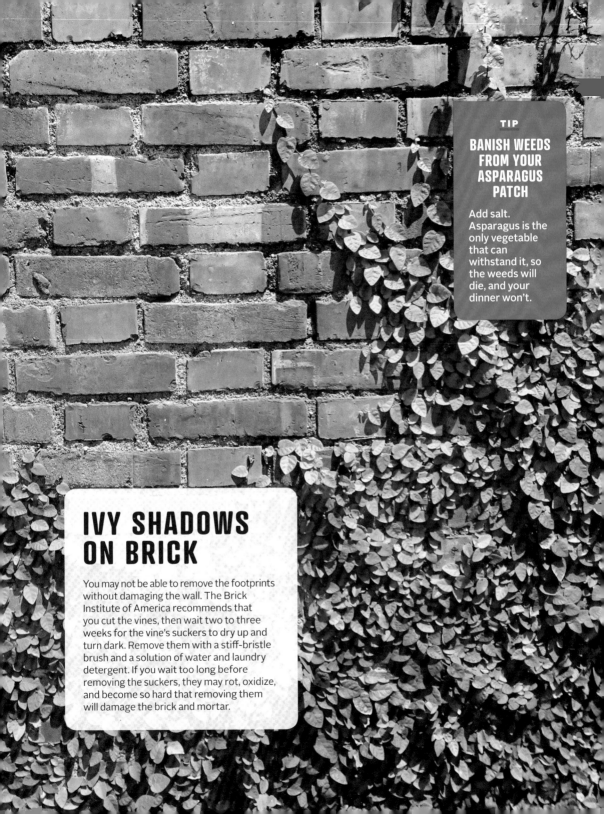

IVY SHADOWS ON BRICK

You may not be able to remove the footprints without damaging the wall. The Brick Institute of America recommends that you cut the vines, then wait two to three weeks for the vine's suckers to dry up and turn dark. Remove them with a stiff-bristle brush and a solution of water and laundry detergent. If you wait too long before removing the suckers, they may rot, oxidize, and become so hard that removing them will damage the brick and mortar.

THE
ESSENTIAL
TOOL

ROUNDNOSE SHOVEL

The roundnose shovel digs, cuts, and pries, but, like any tool, its efficiency depends on you. Start with the shovel perpendicular to the soil, and use your weight and leg muscles, not your arms, to drive it down. To toss dirt, hold the shovel close and keep your forward hand on the blade socket. Bend both knees. If you're right-handed, point your left foot in the direction of the toss.

TREE ROOTS BREAKING UP PATIO PAVERS

Cut a tree root and you risk killing, or at least seriously harming, the tree. Removing one large root may eliminate 25 percent of the tree's total root system. But, if you're careful, you should be able to reduce the risk significantly.

Cut as far from the trunk as possible. To see how close you can go, measure the diameter of the trunk, in inches, at a point 4½ feet above the ground. Then multiply that number by 6. The resulting figure tells you the minimum distance you can cut from the trunk. Pry up the pavers, set them aside, cut through the root using a bow saw, then replace the pavers' substrate. Either use a hand tamper or rent a vibrating plate compactor to pack down the substrate material firmly. When you're finished, you can lay the pavers back in place. And get ready to repeat this process in a few years. Severed roots react by producing large numbers of smaller roots. This compensating growth likely will need to be cut back repeatedly.

ASK ROY

POPULAR MECHANICS' SENIOR HOME EDITOR SOLVES YOUR MOST PRESSING PROBLEMS.

(Q) We get ferocious runoff that damages flower beds and undercuts the driveway. I can't remove the hill that causes it. What can I do about the runoff?

(A) Runoff frustrates many homeowners, and the dirt, wood chips, grass clippings, and debris it scours from the yard can pollute public waters. So we've got two goals here: Divert the water to stop the damage to your property, and slow it down enough so that it percolates into the soil, rather than racing over it. All of the following approaches will work well, depending on the situation.

BUILD A BERM

This small hill, covered with grass or other plants, will divert runoff around what you want to protect. You'll need to think about where the diverted water will flow, then consider what to plant. Grass is easy, until it's time to mow it. A variety of other plantings might be easier to maintain and can help the berm blend into the landscape.

INTERCEPT THE WATER

Try a swale—a shallow ditch with gently sloping sides—or a French drain—a gravel-filled trench that may have a perforated pipe at the bottom. One option is the EZ-Drain, which consists of a perforated pipe and plastic beads encased in a tube of landscape fabric. The fabric surrounds the pipe like a sock and prevents dirt from infiltrating and filling up the pipe or the air spaces between the beads. Because French drains handle water that is moving not just over the soil but through it, they're the best solution for keeping water out of a basement.

ROUTE THE WATER INTO A DRY WELL

This hole in the ground remains dry most of the time. When water is flowing, it can be routed to the well by a swale or roof downspout. Dry wells are particularly helpful in a spot where downspouts are flooding a large paved area or when you're coping with runoff from a large roof. You can also dig a dry well in any low area where a big puddle tends to form.

GRADE BROAD SURFACES

You could also direct runoff away from houses, sheds, barns, and patios. This often requires a professional excavator or expensive rental equipment. But it's almost always an essential step for correcting a flooded basement or crawlspace.

REPLACE IMPERMEABLE SURFACES

Swap a material such as concrete for pavers and gravel. This can be expensive, but it's worth considering, especially if you're already replacing deteriorated asphalt or concrete.

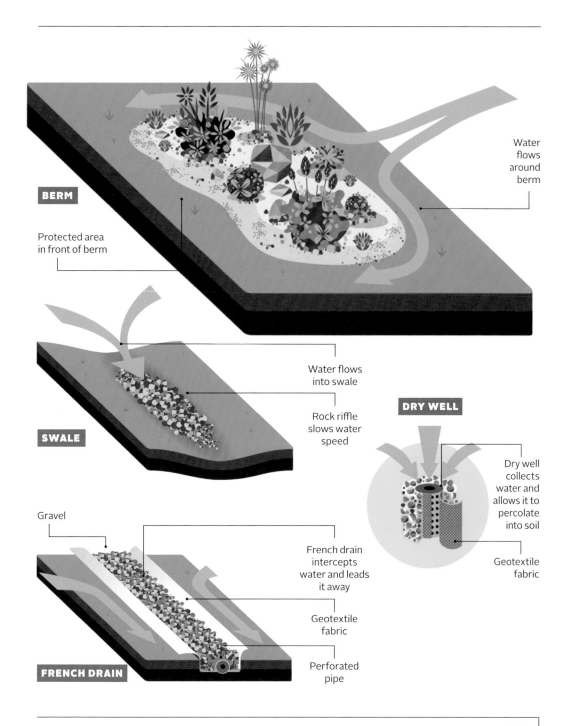

BERM

Water flows around berm

Protected area in front of berm

SWALE

Water flows into swale

Rock riffle slows water speed

DRY WELL

Dry well collects water and allows it to percolate into soil

Geotextile fabric

Gravel

FRENCH DRAIN

French drain intercepts water and leads it away

Geotextile fabric

Perforated pipe

TURNED UP SHINGLES

When the corners of asphalt shingles curl and turn up, the roof deck and undersides of the shingles become vulnerable to water penetration by wind-driven rain. If you don't have too many curling shingles, the job is easy. Resecure any affected shingles with quick-setting asphalt roofing cement. To do this, apply a dab about the size of a quarter under each corner, and press the shingles down so they lie flat. You may have to lay a weighted board over badly curled shingles. This repair should be done on a warm day when the shingles are pliable. Quick-setting roofing cement is available at hardware or roofing supply stores.

Widespread curling, however, indicates that the shingles have dried out and are losing their ability to keep the roof weathertight. In this case, it's hardly worth your time trying to salvage them. The same holds true for your disappearing mineral granules. They are pressed into the asphalt coating of the shingles to provide a fire-resistant surface, color, and protection from the sun's ultraviolet rays. Once most of your shingles have lost their granules, you'll have to reshingle the roof.

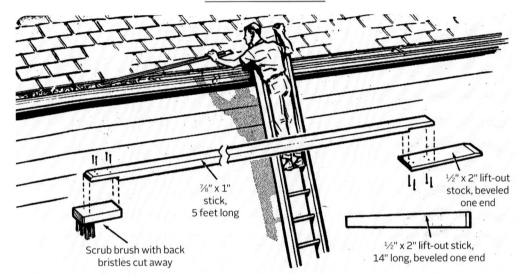

⅞" x 1" stick, 5 feet long

½" x 2" lift-out stock, beveled one end

½" x 2" lift-out stick, 14" long, beveled one end

Scrub brush with back bristles cut away

DIRTY GUTTERS

You can clean the gutters more efficiently by constructing a simple tool to extend your reach and lift more effectively. Take a plank of an appropriate width for your gutter and attach an old scrub brush to one end and a beveled board to the other (or just bevel the plank). Use the brush to gather debris and the bevel to lift it out.

Blisters on Roll Roofing

Blisters are fairly common on a flat roof. They are caused by water that has been trapped under the roofing. As the roof is heated by the sun, the trapped water expands. This raises the roofing and results in a blister. With age and exposure to the sun, the oils in roll roofing materials evaporate, and the roofing becomes brittle. If you accidentally walk on a brittle blister, it will crack. To repair one, cut an X into the blister across its perimeter. Fold the flaps back, exposing the area under the blister. Coat that area with asphalt roofing cement, and then fold the flaps down over the cement. There will be some overlap of the flaps, but try to keep them as flat as possible. Now coat the flaps with roofing cement and embed fiberglass mesh into it. In most cases, by the time blisters develop, the entire roof surface has weathered and is in need of a coating of asphalt emulsion. This helps extend the life of the roofing. In this case, after patching the blister, coat the roof surface according to the directions on the coating container.

STAINS IN VINYL SIDING

STAIN	CLEANERS
BUBBLE GUM	Fantastik, Murphy Oil Soap, Windex, solution of 30% vinegar and 70% water
CRAYON	Lestoil
FELT-TIP PEN	Fantastik, water-based cleaners
GRASS	Fantastik, Lysol, Murphy Oil Soap, Windex
LIPSTICK	Fantastik, Murphy Oil Soap
LITHIUM GREASE	Fantastik, Lestoil, Murphy Oil Soap, Windex
MOLD AND MILDEW	Fantastik, Windex, solution of 30% vinegar and 70% water
MOTOR OIL	Fantastik, Lysol, Murphy Oil Soap, Windex
OIL	Soft Scrub
OIL-BASED CAULK	Fantastik
PAINT	Brillo Pad, Soft Scrub
PENCIL	Soft Scrub
RUST	Fantastik, Murphy Oil Soap, Windex
TAR	Soft Scrub
TOPSOIL	Fantastik, Lestoil, Murphy Oil Soap

ASK ROY

POPULAR MECHANICS' SENIOR HOME EDITOR SOLVES YOUR MOST PRESSING PROBLEMS.

(Q)

The two decorative posts on our front stoop are starting to rot. Are these easy to replace?

(A) Yes. Your first step is to support the roof load. Position a scrap of lumber near the post you want to remove. Jack the scrap piece up using a pair of plastic chain-saw felling wedges nested against each other. Next, drive the wedges together just enough so that the old post dangles freely from the roof assembly. Using the post as a gigantic lever, twist it free from the roof structure. You'll probably have to use a pry bar to coax it completely out. Ideally, you want to remove the post without wrecking it so that you can use it as a pattern to mark the replacement post. Cut the new post and insert it in the same position as the old one. Then gently remove the support lumber by tapping out the wedges to lower the load onto the new post. Repeat with the other post.

Decorative turned posts have a top and a bottom, so make the shortening cut on the same end on both posts (usually the bottom). If you don't do this, you'll produce two posts of the correct length, but the turned section will be at a slightly different height on each. This is visually clumsy. Your neighbors won't let you live it down.

Q: Soil under our concrete-slab front porch has eroded. The slab bridges the gap and there are no cracks in it. Will the slab crack eventually?

A: Yes. Since a slab is only as good as the base it sits on, the cavity should be filled with a slurry mixture of sand and cement, funneled into the gap or rammed into it with a pushrod made of lumber. If you can't get the mixture into the gap because it extends too far under the slab, hire a contractor to pump a grout mixture into the space.

Every summer, moles wreck my yard. What do I do?

Moles burrow after insects in the ground, but eliminating their food source isn't the best approach. You'll end up killing near-surface insects and larvae, some of which—earthworms, for instance—are beneficial. Plus, you'll cause the moles to dig deeper. It's not a bad idea to selectively apply an insecticide to kill turf-destroying insects like grubs. But it won't do much to solve the mole problem. Now, killing near-surface insects and driving the moles deeper does have advantages.

You will no longer see mole tunnels and the critters won't kill off big chunks of your lawn by chewing through grass roots. But as soon as the ground thaws and the near-surface insect population increases, they'll be back. The ugly truth is that traps work best. Just know that killing one or two isn't enough to eliminate the problem. Chances are you'll need to work through the summer and into the fall when they start their deep tunneling. You kill enough of them, you'll have peace—at least for a while.

KNOW
—YOUR—
STUFF

Marking Implements

**A /
NO. 2
PENCIL**
Marks fine lines on softwood and light-colored hardwood for building furniture, cutting trim. But: Tip breaks frequently on rough, heavy-duty jobs.

**B /
CARPEN-
TER'S
PENCIL**
Marks reasonably dry construction lumber. It's rugged. But: Even when sharp, it won't mark fine lines for precise cuts.

**C /
MARKING
KNIFE**
Cuts a very fine line into lumber for furniture construction. But: Since the line is cut, it can't be smudged off or erased. Get the line right the first time.

**D /
INDELIBLE
SHARPIE**
Marks any smooth, light-colored material (lumber, glass, PVC, vinyl, aluminum, brass, copper, or steel). But: Soft tip is easily damaged.

**E /
CARBIDE-
TIP
SCRIBER**
Makes a very fine line on tile and metal (aluminum, copper, brass, high-carbon steel, cast iron). But: Tip cannot be sharpened once dull.

**F /
AWL**
Scribes soft metals (low-carbon steel, copper, brass, aluminum). It can be sharpened. But: Can't readily scribe hard, high-carbon steel and tile.

**G /
SNAPPED-
OFF
HACKSAW
BLADE**
Scores a ragged line into concrete, asphalt, rusted metal. But: The junkyard dog of marking tools, it's not particularly precise.

DAMAGED CEDAR SIDING SHINGLES

Individual cedar shingles on a side wall of a house can be replaced, but if there are large numbers in poor condition (more than a third or so of the wall surface), it may make more sense to strip the wall and reshingle it.

Replacing a few shingles is a pretty straightforward job. To remove a damaged shingle, use a hacksaw to saw through the nails that hold the shingle in place (**1**). A damaged shingle that fits tightly can be split with a chisel. After splitting it and lifting away the pieces, you would still need to use a hacksaw blade to cut off the nails. Try to remove one of the shingles without breaking it, or at least preserve a piece that is large enough to take to the lumberyard to match with a new product. Cedar shingles come in a variety of shapes and sizes, and it's important to match, as closely as possible, the replacements with the existing siding.

To install a replacement shingle, first pretreat it with a water-repellent preservative, stain, or primer. At a minimum, its back and edges should be coated. Next, hold the shingle ½ inch below its finished position and drive a shingle nail into it at about a 45-degree angle (**2**). Butt a wood block to the base of the shingle, then tap the shingle into final position by striking the block with a hammer (**3**). This distorts the nail slightly but the shingle is still held securely in position.

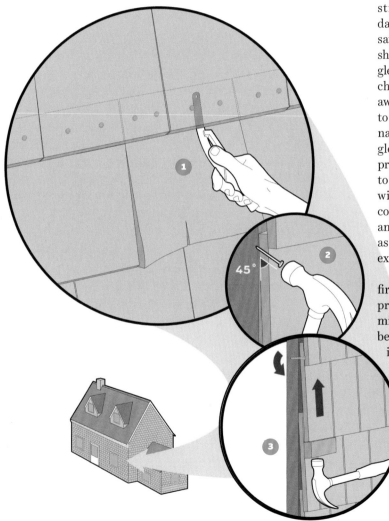

THE MOWER
WON'T START

Before you give up and take it to the repair
shop, take out the spark plug and empty the
gas. Then get a new plug, add some fresh
gas to the tank, and, more often than not,
the mower will start right up.

The Mower Tune-Up

The tune-up interval for a typical small engine on a mower is about 50 hours or once a season, whichever comes first.

1

Scrape the deck.
Disconnect the spark plug and siphon out the fuel tank or remove it, then tip the mower back and give the deck a thorough scraping with a putty knife and a wire brush.

2

Sharpen the blade.
Remove the blade and sharpen it with a mill bastard file. Take off an equal amount of metal from both sides. You can check by balancing the blade on a bolt clamped in a bench vise or by using a store-bought blade balancer. Employ a torque wrench when you reinstall the blade; tighten the blade-retaining bolt according to the specs in the owner's manual.

3

Check the plug.
Install a new, properly gapped plug after 100 hours of operation or once a season, whichever comes first.

4

Service the air filter.
According to engine manufacturer Briggs & Stratton, paper or foam filters should be replaced every 25 hours of operation, while paper filters that have a foam filter precleaner last for 100 hours of operation. Never use compressed air to blow out a paper air cleaner, because you run the risk of perforating the paper.

5

Clean the flywheel.
If your mower sees more than 4 hours of use a week or runs in dusty and dirty conditions, uncover the flywheel at midseason and brush off the fins with an old paintbrush.

BROKEN WINDOWPANE

Wearing thick leather gloves, knock or pull out all the remaining glass. Soften the putty with a hair dryer, then cut it away with a putty knife. Using needle-nose pliers, pull out the glazing points holding the window. Cut the new glass $1/8$ inch undersize, press it into a thin layer of putty, and install new glazing points. Fill up the ledge outside the glass with new putty. Use the V blade on a double-end glazing tool to form the putty neatly into shape, making a smooth transition between the frame and the window. Let it dry two weeks and paint.

Leaf Stains on the Deck

Those stains are caused by tannins leached out of the leaves by rainwater. If the deck is sealed or finished, they'll fade on their own, usually within a couple of weeks. But if the wood is unfinished, hasten the process with a cleaning. If your deck is built with composite lumber, follow the manufacturer's maintenance instructions to avoid surface damage (and voiding your warranty). For example, Trex decking recommends using a cleaner containing oxalic or phosphoric acid. For pressure-treated decking, any jug of cleaner that's rated for decks or fences will work. Next spring do yourself a favor and pressure-wash the deck and apply a stain or sealer. You won't have to deal with this again.

ASK ROY

POPULAR MECHANICS' SENIOR HOME EDITOR SOLVES YOUR MOST PRESSING PROBLEMS.

Every year the stain on my deck peels off. What am I doing wrong?

A Most stains absorb into the wood surface, so they don't form a film that could peel off. They just weather away. The deck was likely either painted or it received multiple coats of stain. Both are bad ideas, because they don't allow the wood to breathe.

What you need to do is use a professional-grade wood stripper, such as Flood Pro Series. Apply it straight out of the bottle, let it stand for half an hour, scrub with a deck brush, and then pressure-wash the deck. It may take several applications to remove the old coating. Complete the job with a coat of high-quality semi-transparent stain. Flood also makes an ideal product for these applications: a semitransparent alkyd/oil stain formulated to soak in and bond, not just adhere to the top layer.

Q: My storm door was ripped open by the wind, damaging the doorjamb. How do I fix it, and how do I prevent this from happening again?

A: Storm doors blow open when their closers are worn out or were not properly installed. So in the course of the repair, you'll want to put in new ones—maybe even a heavy-duty model with more pulling force. The toughest fix is the doorjamb itself. If it's badly cracked, you'll have to either replace the entire thing or saw away the damaged section using an oscillating multitool. The replacement pieces need to be planed to thickness and ripped to width. Each piece should be crosscut to make a tight fit, then fastened with exterior-grade wood screws. Finally, sand the entire jamb, prime, and paint it.

Install a safety chain. It may look ugly, but it reduces the likelihood of damage should the door be ripped open by another gust.

WEATHERED PICNIC TABLES

Begin with an application of an exterior wood cleaner that contains oxalic acid, such as Flood Wood Cleaner. Scrub the table with a coarse synthetic brush, being careful not to score the surfaces. You can use a putty knife or a painter's 5-in-1 tool to remove any gunk that's built up between boards. Now rinse everything and let it all dry. Next, sand off splinters and flatten dents with 120-grit sandpaper. Brush off any dust and gently wipe the surface with a tack cloth (a sticky piece of cheesecloth sold in the paint-supply aisle of hardware stores and home centers). The last step before refinishing is to replace any rusty screws or bolts with some made of hot-dipped galvanized steel. These will have a thick

zinc coating that provides longer-lasting corrosion protection than the whisper-thin plating of zinc or cadmium you find on the bolts and wood screws that come in most home center bins. You can get hot-dipped galvanized fasteners on the web or from old-fashioned hardware stores or industrial supply houses. Finally, apply your finish. A semitransparent stain would be a good choice in that it will provide protection but also allow some of the wood grain to show through. Using a synthetic brush, apply the finish down the length of each board without stopping, so you don't get lap marks. If the picnic table sees harsh sun, you may want to apply two coats and reapply the stain every two to three years.

Broken Tent Pole

Splint it with a branch. You can use medical tape, dental floss, or duct tape.

HEARSTBOOKS

An Imprint of Sterling Publishing Co., Inc.
1166 Avenue of the Americas
New York, NY 10036

ISBN 978-1-61837-260-4

Distributed in Canada by Sterling Publishing Co., Inc.
c/o Canadian Manda Group, 664 Annette Street
Toronto, Ontario, M6S 2C8, Canada
Distributed in the United Kingdom by GMC Distribution Services
Castle Place, 166 High Street, Lewes, East Sussex, BN7 1XU, England
Distributed in Australia by NewSouth Books
45 Beach Street, Coogee, NSW 2034, Australia

For information about custom editions, special sales, and premium and corporate purchases,
please contact Sterling Special Sales at 800-805-5489 or specialsales@sterlingpublishing.com.

Manufactured in Canada

4 6 8 10 9 7 5 3

sterlingpublishing.com
popularmechanics.com

Cover and interior design by Zachary Gilyard
Photography credits on page 191